D0183553

Paul Duncan

ALFRED HITCHCOCK

Architect of Anxiety 1899–1980

TASCHEN

KÜLN LONDON LOS ANGELES MADRID PARIS TOKYO

FRONT COVER
Publicity still for 'The Birds' (1963)
Melanie Daniels (Tippi Hedren) is attacked by birds
and is severely traumatised by the ordeal.

PAGE 1
Alfred Hitchcock's iconic self-portrait.

FRONTISPIECE
Alfred Hitchcock (1966)
Alfred Hitchcock, the voyeur, looks at us.

THIS PAGE
1 **Alfred J. Hitchcock (1924)** A portrait of the artist as
a young man. 2 Alma Hitchcock brings some much-
needed tea to Alfred in his study. 3 **On the set of 'The Lady
Vanishes' (1938)** Hitchcock enjoys the company of Sally
Stewart, Margaret Lockwood and Googie Withers.

OPPOSITE PAGE
On the set of 'Frenzy' (1972)

PAGES 6/7
On the set of 'Rear Window' (1954)
The film was shot on a single set. This image gives some
idea of the technology and the number of people involved
in the production. Alfred Hitchcock can be seen in the
centre watching James Stewart on the far left.

BACK COVER
On the set of 'Psycho' (1960)
Alfred Joseph Hitchcock.

© 2003 TASCHEN GmbH
Hohenzollernring 53, D-50672 Köln
www.taschen.com
Editor/Layout: Paul Duncan/Wordsmith Solutions
Typeface Design: Sense/Net, Andy Disl, Cologne

Printed in Italy
ISBN 3-8228-1591-8

Notes
A superscript number indicates a reference to a note on page 191.

Images
British Film Institute Stills, Posters and Designs, London: 4left, 5, 8, 11 (4), 12 (4),
15top right+bottom left+bottom right, 17tl+b, 18, 21, 22, 24 (2), 26 (2), 27, 28
(2), 29 (2), 30b, 32, 33, 34, 35, 36, 37 (2), 38, 39, 40 (2), 41 (2), 42 (3), 43,
44, 46, 47t, 48, 49, 50/51, 52, 54/55, 56 (2), 57 (2), 58, 59 (2), 60t, 61, 62, 63
(2), 64 (2), 65b, 66b, 67, 68/69, 70, 72 (2), 73, 74, 75, 76, 77 (2), 79, 84, 85,
88 (2), 89, 90, 91, 93bl+br, 98, 99, 102tl+tr, 104 (2), 105, 107t, 108b, 115 (3),
121tl+tr, 123, 124tl+tr+br, 126t, 127b, 130–133 (3, 9, 13, 15, 16, 18, 19, 20,
21, 23, 27, 34, 35), 140 (2), 142, 144 (2), 145, 148, 149, 151 (2), 153t, 154,
158b, 160, 161b, 162, 170, 171t, 173b, 176, 177, 178b, 179 (2), 182, 185tr,
185bl, 186b, 187tr, 188t, 189l, 190 (3)
PWE Verlag/defd-movies, Hamburg: 4middle, 6/7, 15tl, 17tr, 66t, 116, 121b, 126b,
127t, 129, 130–133 (5, 6, 8, 24, 25, 26, 28, 29, 30, 31, 36), 147b, 152, 155,
173t, Back Cover
Herbert Klemens/Filmbild Fundus Robert Fischer, Munich: 1, 45, 47b, 80, 93t,
102b, 107b, 130–133 (12), 141, 147t, 156/157, 158t, 180/181
The Kobal Collection, London/New York: 60b, 71, 78, 86/87, 120, 128, 130–133
(1, 7, 10), 139, 146, 153b, 161t, 171b, 172, 174, 175, 178t
Timepix, New York: 82 (Gjon Mili), 94 (J.R. Eyerman), 95 (J.R. Eyerman), 96/97
(J.R. Eyerman), 100/101 (Gjon Mili), 103 (John Florea), 117 (Bob Landry),
134/135 (Eliot Elisofon)
Magnum, London/New York/Paris: 110 (Robert Capa), 111 (Robert Capa), 112
(Robert Capa), 113 (Robert Capa), 136 (Philippe Halsman), Cover and 166
(Philippe Halsman), 192 (Philippe Halsman)
Hulton Getty Archive, London: 30t (Evening Standard), 81 (Kurt Hutton/Picture
Post), 106 (Madison Lacy/John Kobal Foundation), 114 (John Miehle), 122
(Picture Post)
Corbis: 2 (Hulton-Deutsch Collection), 108t (John Springer Collection), 138 (John
Springer Collection), 143b (Underwood & Underwood)
MPTV, Los Angeles: 118/119, 143t, 168/169

Copyright
The film images in this book are copyright to the respective distributors: D.R.
Emelka GBA (*The Pleasure Garden*), Gainsborough (*The Mountain Eagle, The
Lodger, Downhill, Easy Virtue, Young and Innocent, The Lady Vanishes*), British
International Pictures (*The Ring, The Manxman, The Farmer's Wife, Champagne,
Blackmail, Juno and the Paycock, Murder!, The Skin Game, Number Seventeen,
Rich and Strange*), Tom Arnold Productions (*Waltzes from Vienna*), Gaumont British
Pictures (*The Man Who Knew Too Much* (1934), *The 39 Steps, Secret Agent,
Sabotage, Young and Innocent*), Verity Films (*Jamaica Inn*), David O. Selznick
(*Rebecca, Spellbound, The Paradine Case*), United Artists (*Foreign Correspondent*),
RKO (*Mr & Mrs Smith*), Fox (*Lifeboat*), Transatlantic Pictures (*Rope, Under
Capricorn*), Universal (*Saboteur, Shadow of a Doubt, The Trouble with Harry, Rear
Window, To Catch a Thief, The Man Who Knew Too Much* (1956), *Vertigo, Psycho,
The Birds, Marnie, Torn Curtain, Topaz, Frenzy, Family Plot*), Disney (*Notorious*),
Warner Brothers (*Strangers on a Train, Stage Fright, I Confess, Dial M for Murder,
The Wrong Man*), Turner Entertainment (*North by Northwest*), Aries (*Suspicion*). We
deeply regret it if, despite our concerted efforts, any copyright owners have been
unintentionally overlooked and omitted. Obviously we will amend any such errors in
the next edition if they are brought to the attention of the publisher.

Introduction:
Fear of Falling

In the early part of his film career, Alfred Hitchcock met with a small group of friends to complain about people and events within the film industry. They called themselves The Hate Club. It was an informal way for them to vent their frustrations, but it was also a useful way for them to learn from each other. On one occasion, they each had to answer the question 'Who do you make films for?' The other film-makers said "the distributors" or "the audience" but Hitchcock was reticent to answer. Eventually he said, "the press." He reasoned that it was they who influenced the audience who, in turn, influenced the distributors and exhibitors. Further, Hitchcock said, "We [the directors] make a film succeed. The name of the director should be associated in the public's mind with a quality product. Actors come and actors go, but the name of the director should stay clearly in the mind of the audiences."

Hitchcock acted upon this assertion throughout his film career by regularly wining and dining film critics, giving candid interviews and writing more than 60 articles for film and news publications. (At one dinner, a critic apologised to Hitchcock for giving him a bad review some weeks earlier. Hitchcock told her not to worry because she had her job to do and he had his.) His persistent and professional self-promotion (his name appeared above the title of his films, he often appeared in cameos within his films and he introduced a long-running *Alfred Hitchcock Presents* TV series in the 1950s) led to him becoming one of the most well-known film-makers of his generation. Also, when film criticism and theory were being developed in the 1960s, everybody used Hitchcock films like *Rear Window*, *Vertigo*, *North by Northwest* and *Psycho* as examples because, as David Thomson pointed out, these films 'are deeply expressive of the way we watch and respond to stories… Thus Hitchcock became a way of defining film, a man exclusively intent on the moving image and the compulsive emotions of the spectator.'[1]

When interviewed, Hitchcock enthusiastically explained the practical and technical details of his work. Jules Dassin, who was sent to learn from Hitchcock on the set of *Mr & Mrs Smith*, remembered a lunch over which Hitchcock explained the basic camera angles and techniques of film-making, drawing on napkins to

On the set of 'To Catch a Thief' (1955)
Hitchcock holds onto a pole in the centre foreground whilst filming the climactic rooftop chase. (See also pages 16 and 142.)

Hitchcock called writer John Michael Hayes to the top of the 'To Catch a Thief' set and told him, "Everybody down there is thinking that I have called you up here to talk about something profound in the script, but I really wanted to find out if you were as scared of heights as I am."

"My wife cooks every night, and I help her wash up."

Alfred Hitchcock

Deadlier than the male
Hitchcock's icy blondes sometimes resorted to violence.

OPPOSITE TOP
Still from 'North by Northwest' (1959)
Eve Kendall (Eva Marie Saint) shoots Roger Thornhill (Cary Grant) in front of the implacable gaze of the presidents at Mount Rushmore.

OPPOSITE BOTTOM LEFT
Still from 'Blackmail' (1929)
Alice (Anny Ondra) kills a man who was trying to rape her.

OPPOSITE BOTTOM MIDDLE
Still from 'Marnie' (1964)
Marnie (Tippi Hedren) must shoot her horse after it falls.

OPPOSITE BOTTOM RIGHT
Publicity still for 'Secret Agent' (1936)
Madeleine Carroll.

make it clear to Dassin. Hitchcock also talked at length to reporters, biographers and TV presenters about his meticulously prepared screenplays and storyboards, making it sound as though filming with actors was a mere formality. Director George Cukor was not convinced this was the case. In 1964 he said that Hitchcock "is an absolute master… But between you and me I'm not quite sure that he is telling the complete truth. He must improvise with performances sometimes. There was a picture of his called *Suspicion* where Joan Fontaine gave the most extraordinary performance. Now, I can't believe that that was all mechanical – all planned… He is hiding things from you; he doesn't say how he works, how he achieves effects – easier to say it was all planned in the script and the rest is mechanics."[2]

Hitchcock compared the preparation process to a composer writing his score for musicians to play. In the same way that the composer can hear the music before it is played, Hitchcock could see and hear the film in his head. Once this was clear, then he could try to turn it into a reality with sets, cameramen, actors and editors. It is probable that Hitchcock loved the pre-production process because the film was still pure inside his head. As friend and interviewer Peter Bogdanovich noted, 'shooting was the area of compromise, to his mind, and of potential confrontation.' However, Hitchcock was not as in control and as certain of the end result as he wanted us to believe. As ably demonstrated in Bill Krohn's *Hitchcock at Work* and Dan Auiler's *Hitchcock's Notebooks*, on some films the script was still being rewritten during filming, the storyboards were often used by production designers to show how a scene would look rather than as it would be filmed, and Hitchcock worked with actors and crew to adapt his vision to the screen. This need for compromise must have played havoc with Hitchcock's need for control. On *Suspicion*, for example, the ending of the film was changed many times before the final, last-minute one was inserted. And according to Joan Fontaine, who starred in Hitchcock's *Rebecca* and won an Oscar for her performance in *Suspicion*, she talked to other actors and they came to the conclusion that Hitchcock operated a 'divide and rule' attitude to actors – he would alienate the main actors from each other and then direct them individually. This gave Hitchcock more control over their performances. 'He wanted total loyalty, but only to him,' Fontaine wrote.[3] Compare this to legendary costume designer Edith Head's comment: "Loyalty was extremely important to Alfred Hitchcock. He was as loyal to his craftsmen as he expected them to be to him." Hitchcock worked repeatedly with many of the crew (and actors) and this gave him a safe, controllable environment within which to make some of his finest films in the 1950s and early 1960s.

By concentrating upon the technical aspects of his work, Hitchcock presented himself as an artisan and master craftsman. He told Peter Bogdanovich, "You've got to know your craft in order to express the art,"[4] but did not consider himself an artist. When asked about the subtext of his work, he told *Movie* that "I'm more interested in the technique of story telling by means of film rather than in what film contains."[5] He preferred to paint broad strokes when explaining his work – he said that *The Birds* was about "too much complacency in the world: that people are unaware that catastrophe surrounds us all."[6] Many friends attribute Hitchcock's reluctance to talk in detail about his work as an indication that he did not understand his own films, that he lacked self-knowledge. Rather than

analyse his own work, he delighted in titillating his readers with references to the sexual undertones of his films like the recurring fetish of handcuffs and the delicious sexual pleasures behind the icy exteriors of his blonde female characters. The copious interviews, including François Truffaut's reverential booklong interview, reveal little about Hitchcock's personal concerns. He expresses no spiritual or political opinions. I suspect that Hitchcock's innate need for privacy and control would have been compromised if he had revealed his innermost desires in the public arena, so he simply used his wit and store of anecdotes to deflect attention away from the substance of his life.

Hitchcock had three personas: public, professional and private. The public persona was the practical joker and cynical clown, who appeared on film posters, in cameos within the films and in introductions to his long-running TV show. John Russell Taylor, Hitchcock's friend and official biographer, wrote that Hitchcock's professional persona 'turns all his energies to the preparation of a film, calculates everything in advance down to the last detail and throws himself totally into the meticulous realisation of his plans; the man of routine and strict discipline, the still centre of confident purposefulness on set, the man who never has to raise his voice, never show anger, to the extent that he believes he cannot even feel anger.'[7] Hitchcock's private persona was a quiet family man, who went to church every Sunday with his daughter, who completely adored his wife, who collected original art by Paul Klee, Walter Sickert and others, who was proud of his wine collection and who tried out all the best restaurants before settling on one and sticking to it.

Although he worked with a restricted palette of emotions, Hitchcock mastered his film-making craft as only a few before him. His subject was suspense and he tried to construct plots so that the audience were kept in a state of suspense for as long a period as possible. He explained the mechanics of suspense quite succinctly: "If you touch off a bomb, your audience gets a ten-second shock. But if the audience knows that the bomb has been planted, then you can build up the suspense and keep them in a state of expectation for five minutes."[8] Hitchcock was, without doubt, the best architect of anxiety the cinema has ever seen but does this skill alone merit his reputation? Pauline Kael, the doyenne of film criticism, wrote: 'It could even be argued, I think, that Hitchcock's uniformity, his mastery of tricks, and his cleverness at getting audiences to respond according to his calculations – the feedback he wants and gets from them – reveal not so much a personal style as a personal theory of audience psychology, that his methods and approach are not those of an artist but a prestidigitator.'[9]

Was Hitchcock nothing more than a clever conjuror?

"Despite all my bluster and bravado, I'm really quite sensitive and cowardly."

Alfred Hitchcock

Chained
Handcuffs, chains and ropes are used repeatedly to force people together. Also see the images on pages 29, 62, 63 and 65.

OPPOSITE TOP LEFT
Still from 'The 39 Steps' (1935)
Pamela (Madeleine Carroll) tries to unhitch herself from Richard Hannay (Robert Donat), who is on the run for murder.

OPPOSITE TOP RIGHT
Still from 'Number Seventeen' (1932)
Rose (Anne Grey) and Allardyce (John Stuart) are tied together.

OPPOSITE BOTTOM LEFT
Still from 'The Wrong Man' (1956)
Manny Balestrero (Henry Fonda) contemplates the injustice done to him.

OPPOSITE BOTTOM RIGHT
Still from 'The Mountain Eagle' (1926)
Beatrice (Nita Naldi) looks on aghast as Fear o' God Fulton (Malcolm Keen) is suddenly handcuffed whilst winding wool.

"Self-plagiarism is style."

Alfred Hitchcock

Vertigo
Many pivotal moments in Hitchcock's films involve high places or the possibility of falling. Also see images on pages 61, 66, 74, 100/101, 142 and 154.

OPPOSITE TOP LEFT
Still from 'To Catch a Thief' (1955)
John Robie (Cary Grant) tries to capture the cat burglar impersonating him.

OPPOSITE TOP RIGHT
Still from 'North by Northwest' (1959)
Roger Thornhill (Cary Grant) and Eve Kendall (Eva Marie Saint) try to escape the spies via Mount Rushmore.

OPPOSITE BOTTOM LEFT
Still from 'Blackmail' (1929)
Tracy (Donald Calthrop) the blackmailer is pursued through the British Museum after being framed for a killing.

OPPOSITE BOTTOM RIGHT
Still from 'Young and Innocent' (1937)
Robert (Derrick de Marney) and Old Will (Edward Rigby) hold onto Erica (Nova Pilbeam) when their car falls into a mine shaft. John Woo later reused the idea in 'Broken Arrow' (1996).

Hitchcock once said: "I don't put my personal feelings into pictures." When approaching an analysis of Hitchcock's films, and indeed any story, it is best to apply D. H. Lawrence's advice: 'Never trust the teller. Trust the tale.' The thoughts and concerns of the teller are woven into the tale, whether the teller knows it or not.

In *The Interpretation of Dreams*, Sigmund Freud wrote, 'Dreams of falling are more frequently characterised by anxiety.' Hitchcock must have been very anxious because as James Wolcott wrote, 'Of all his motifs and signature strokes (staircases, keys, birds), the one I find most intriguing is his fascination with falling. Steep falls were his dramatic crescendos.'[10] A quick survey of Hitchcock's films reveals mainly vertiginous situations: on the British Museum in *Blackmail*; on a cliff in *Secret Agent*, *Suspicion* and *Spellbound*; falling into a mine shaft in *Young and Innocent*; on the rigging in *Jamaica Inn*; on the Statue of Liberty in *Saboteur*; falling from the eponymous *Rear Window*; on the roof in *To Catch a Thief*; on Mount Rushmore in *North by Northwest*; and Arbogast falling down the stairs in *Psycho*. Wolcott points out, 'The falls are usually photographed from a high angle, the camera often focusing on hands clutching one another for dear life, the figure dropping or about to drop into a whirlpool abyss.'[11]

The falling motif was central to the plot of *Vertigo*, where Scottie's fear of heights is used against him. The subtext is that Scottie is afraid of committing to relationships (of falling in love), a common male trait, as observed in *Rear Window*, *North by Northwest* and *To Catch a Thief*. After the death of his idealised love, Madeleine Elster, Scottie uses Judy Barton to obsessively build a replica of his ideal, unaware that Madeleine and Judy are the same person. Just as he overcomes his anxiety about committing to the replica, he discovers Judy's deceit and loses her for a second and final time. She falls for him, both figuratively and literally.

Hitchcock used the tension of opposites to create anxiety in the viewer, as *Vertigo* demonstrates. In the first half the viewer, like Scottie, is seduced by the elaborate, entwining love story. However, in the second half, we both fear and empathise with Scottie's monstrous actions. It is Hitchcock who has used his technical skill to seduce the viewer into the mind of a madman. As David Thomson noted, 'Hitchcock's most profound subject and achievement is the juxtaposition of sanity and insanity, of bourgeois ordinariness and criminal outrage.'[12] Many insane monsters have been featured strongly in Hitchcock's movies, including Uncle Charlie in *Shadow of a Doubt*, Bruno Anthony in *Strangers on a Train*, Norman Bates in *Psycho* and Bob Rusk in *Frenzy*. If Hitchcock's insane monsters owe a debt to Peter Lorre's child sex murderer in Fritz Lang's *M*, then his usual villains – the criminal mastermind who is also a respected member of the community – are also reminiscent of Lang's *Dr Mabuse* films.

Hitchcock loved to play with the conventions of the thriller format. Instead of having dark, solitary settings for his stories of suspense and murder, he preferred light, humorous, crowded places where murder could hide in plain sight. The villain would have a wife and children. "I think that murder should be done on a lovely summer's day by a babbling brook," Hitchcock said. "The liveliest fellow at a party might well be a psychopathic killer."[13] Critic Andrew Sarris explains further, 'Hitchcock requires a situation of normality, however dull it may seem on the surface, to emphasise the evil abnormality that lurks beneath the surface.

"I believe in pure cinema."

Alfred Hitchcock[4]

Hitchcock understands, as his detractors do not, the crucial function of counterpoint in the cinema.'[14]

Hitchcock also understood how to compose clean and dynamic images for the two-dimensional screen, as well as design sophisticated and precise patterns of visual motifs. To Hitchcock, "The cinema is a succession of images put together like a sentence. Together they tell a story."[15] He very much believed in the discipline of the pure cinema that developed at the end of the silent era and preferred to tell stories through images and sounds rather than with dialogue. In Sarris' words, 'Like [John] Ford, Hitchcock cuts in his mind, and not in the cutting room with five different set-ups for every scene. His is the only style that unites the divergent classical traditions of [F. W.] Murnau (camera movement) and [Sergei] Eisenstein (montage)… Unfortunately, Hitchcock seldom receives the visual analysis he deserves.'[16]

There are many sequences in Hitchcock's work where he uses the movement of the camera combined with editing to put the viewer in the position of his characters. By seeing what the characters see, the viewer empathises with them. You see a character on the screen looking at something, you see what they see (you in their position), then you see the character react to that something. In *The Lodger*, the Bunting family look up at their ceiling to see the light fittings shake, then we are looking up at the ceiling, at the light fittings shaking, the ceiling made of glass and watching the lodger walking up and down. (See picture on page 29.) In *Rear Window*, we are in the position of Jeff, realising something is wrong, but not being able to do anything about it, being helpless in the wheelchair, as we are helpless in our cinema seats. In *Psycho*, we are Norman Bates, looking through a hole in the wall at Marion Crane undressing. In this film, more than any other, we are both the villain and the hero, able to switch sides, to satisfy both our civilised and uncouth instincts. According to Robin Wood, 'Hitchcock's complex and disconcerting moral sense, in which good and evil seem to be so interwoven as to be virtually inseparable … insists on the existence of evil impulses in all of us,' and Hitchcock makes us 'aware, perhaps not quite at the conscious level (it depends on the spectator), of the impurity of our own desires.'[17] We don't just watch his films, we participate in them. As Hitch said, "We are all criminals, we who watch. We are all Peeping Toms. And we follow the Eleventh Commandment: 'Thou shalt not be found out.'" Hitchcock then generates suspense in his movies by having us believe that our impure desires will be found out.

Hitchcock's strength as a film-maker was that he was able to visualise his subconscious fears and desires and turn them into waking nightmares on the silver screen. Many viewers share his subconscious fears and desires, which is why he will remain in the public consciousness for many years to come.

Strangling
Hitchcock always maintained that strangling was the best way to kill somebody because you only need your hands. Also see images on pages 26, 81, 99, 117 and 124.

OPPOSITE TOP LEFT
Still from 'Dial M for Murder' (1954)
Margot Wendice (Grace Kelly) is attacked by Lesgate (Anthony Dawson) upon the orders of her husband.

OPPOSITE TOP RIGHT
Still from 'Strangers on a Train' (1951)
Psychopath Bruno Anthony (Robert Walker) loses control during a genteel dinner party.

OPPOSITE BOTTOM
Still from 'Frenzy' (1972)
Brenda Blaney (Barbara Leigh-Hunt) is strangled with a necktie by charming Bob Rusk.

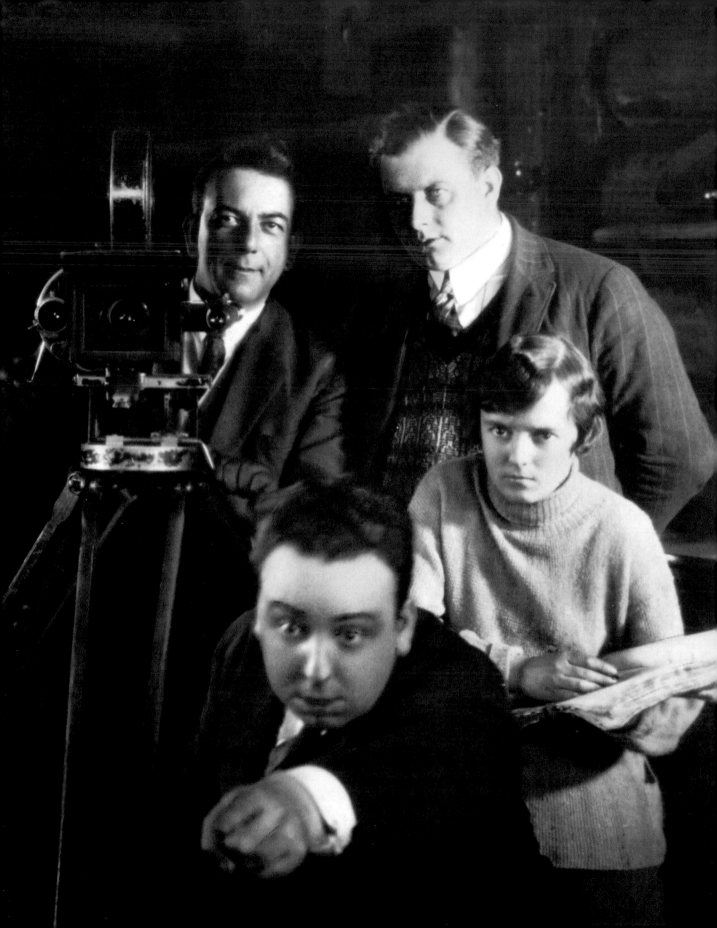

'A Young Man with a Master Mind' 1899–1939

Alfred Joseph Hitchcock was born to William and Emma Hitchcock on 13 August 1899 in Leytonstone, in the East End of London. Alfred was seven years younger than sister Nellie, and nine years younger than his brother William. This age difference left Alfred feeling a little left out when it came to playing with his siblings, so he pursued mainly solitary hobbies to occupy his formative years. His feeling of apartness was not helped when, late one Christmas Eve, he spied his mother taking toys out of his Christmas stocking and putting them into his brother and sister's stockings.

Although the young Alfred was quiet and well-behaved, there is an apocryphal story (told so often by Hitchcock that he forgot whether it was true or not) that when he was five or six he committed some minor nuisance that resulted in his father sending Hitchcock to the police station with a note. The policeman read the note, then locked Hitchcock in a cell for five minutes. Upon release, Hitchcock was told that this is what they do to naughty little boys. Hitchcock later said that this was one root for his fear of authority figures. His school experiences may have also augmented this fear. The Salesian College in Battersea purged the physical and spiritual ills of its pupils with laxatives after the evening meal, with the inevitable consequences. Later, at Saint Ignatius College, Stamford Hill, the Jesuit priests added a psychological dimension to corporal punishment by allowing the children to choose the moment when they would receive their strokes of the hard rubber cane.

It is easy to see how this disciplined regime, combined with his strict Roman Catholic upbringing and a domineering mother, engendered in the young Alfred the certainty that every minor infringement he perpetrated would be immediately and severely punished. He had a keen sense of the boundary between right and wrong, and he was loath to step over it. To help himself stay on the straight and narrow, Hitchcock developed self-control and became highly organised. Although not gifted in any of his academic subjects, he did enjoy geography, and this showed itself in his private study of the London bus network and timetable – he was proud to have ridden on every bus route in London. This intense study extended to him memorising the streets of New York and every stop on the Orient Express railway.

Publicity still for 'The Mountain Eagle' (1926)
For many years this posed image of the young Hitchcock 'directing' in the foreground was the only known picture from the film. Alma Reville, the future Mrs Hitchcock, is taking notes.

"The cinema is not a slice of life, it's a piece of cake"
Alfred Hitchcock

'Doesn't every text return to Oedipus? To tell a story; doesn't this always mean to search out an origin, to clear up relations with the law, to enter into the dialectic of tenderness and hate…'

Roland Barthes, 'Le plaisir du texte'

Hitch left Saint Ignatius College in 1913 and then spent his time watching movies and stage plays as well as educating himself by attending various night classes. It was as though he was groping for some direction in his life – how many fourteen-year-olds have a clear vision of their future career? Hitch started his first job in 1915, as a technical clerk at Henley Telegraph and Cable Company. He was easily bored by this repetitive job and so he would do other things for long periods and then catch up in a burst of fantastic energy. His manager was impressed, until he received complaints from customers about late estimates during Hitch's periodic bouts of boredom. When Hitch took a night class on art history, he began drawing and was transferred to the advertising department at Henley's, where he worked all hours of the day and night consumed by the tasks at hand. He had, at last, found work he enjoyed and had an aptitude for.

In his spare time, the young Hitchcock read the best-selling fiction of the day and eagerly devoured the work of authors John Buchan, G.K. Chesterton and Gustave Flaubert. However, it was the work of Edgar Allen Poe that made the biggest and most lasting impression. Hitch considered Poe to have influenced the romantic novelists, crime and detection fiction as well as being the crucible of the surrealist movement in its diverse forms. Poe's influence on Hitchcock can be seen in 'Gas,' a short story Hitch wrote for the first issue (June 1918) of *The Henley*, the company's social magazine. The story features a woman on the run from an unnamed pursuer, falling deeper into the seedy side of London, from one bad situation to another, on the point of death, then… she regains consciousness, her tooth pulled and owing the dentist half a crown.

The fiction of Poe was related to another of Hitchcock's passions: murder. Hitch was fascinated by true crime and avidly read the lurid reports in the tabloids, visited the Black Museum at Scotland Yard, attended murder trials at the Old Bailey and put all the information from his investigations into notebooks. There were many sensational cases in his local area when he was growing up – the unsolved Jack the Ripper murders of 1888 were still a source of fear and intense speculation in the East End. The closeness and mundanity of murder was brought home to Hitch in 1922 during his study of the Thompson/Bywater murder case, when he realised that four years previously he had been taught ballroom dancing by Edith Thompson's father.

Hitch avidly read all the film trade magazines – *The Motion Picture Herald, The Bioscope, The Kinematograph Lantern Weekly*, etc. – as well as attend the films of D.W. Griffiths, Buster Keaton, Douglas Fairbanks, Jr. and the latest French and German productions. He preferred the technically advanced American films that used light to make the images three-dimensional rather than the flat British pictures. In 1919, Hitch learned through one of the trade magazines that the American film production company Famous Players-Lasky had opened a studio in London and their first film was *The Sorrows of Satan* (1926). He bought Marie Corelli's novel, drew designs for title-cards and submitted them with his portfolio. The film was cancelled, so Hitch tried again with designs for other forthcoming films and was hired, first part-time and then full-time, to design the title-cards for silent films.

Famous Players-Lasky imported some of their top American talent into the London studio, including Eve Unsell, Margaret Turnbull and Ouida Bergere in the editorial department. At that time, it was customary for women to write and

517 The High Road, Leytonstone (circa 1906)
William Hitchcock (left) proudly displays Alfred J. Hitchcock on a horse in front of the family store and home.

edit movies and these three women knew everything there was to know about adapting pre-existing plays and novels into a film scenario. Hitchcock learned about storytelling from them and similarly learned much about directing from the various directors who worked at Famous Players Lasky.

Hitchcock made himself indispensable at the studio, learning every aspect of film-making as well as designing the title-cards. He was regarded as somebody who could be relied on to get the job done, so it was no surprise that he was asked to direct a short comedy variously called *Number Thirteen* and *Mrs Peabody*. It was never completed because Famous Players-Lasky was losing money and had to stop producing films. Instead, they began renting out the studio and technicians to other productions. For one of these short films, *Always Tell Your Wife* (1923), Hitch was assisting the director Hugh Croise when Croise was fired by producer/actor/writer Seymour Hicks. Hicks asked Hitch to co-direct the remaining scenes with him. Producer Michael Balcon and director Graham Cutts made *Woman to Woman* (1923) at the studio and employed Hitch as assistant director. They needed help, so Hitch volunteered to also write the script and do the art direction – the resultant film was a smash hit. The team continued together on four, less successful, films, during which time Balcon took over the studio.

During the production of *Woman to Woman* Hitchcock telephoned Miss Alma Reville at home and asked her if she would like to edit the picture. Hitch had known Alma for two years whilst she had been an editor at the studio, but she held a higher position than him so he felt it had not been proper for him to talk to her. Now that he was in a higher position he arranged for them to work together – Hitch later admitted that he would look at her all the time when she wasn't looking. Alma and Hitch enjoyed each other's company when they went with the production to film *The Blackguard* at Ufa studios in Berlin. It was to prove a turning-point in Hitch's artistic development.

Ufa studios were at the heart of Expressionistic film-making and home to some of the best technicians in the world. Hitchcock, who loved the work of Fritz Lang, Ernst Lubitsch and others, was in seventh heaven watching and talking with F.W. Murnau whilst he was making his masterpiece *Der Letzte Mann* (*The Last Laugh*, 1924) – a silent film that used the visuals to tell the story without a single title-card. With director Graham Cutts absent due to his sexual peccadilloes, Hitchcock put his new-found technical knowledge into practice when he was forced to take over the direction of various scenes.

Buoyed with confidence, on the ship home Hitch proposed marriage to Alma. Alma was seasick in her cabin and in reply, Hitch reported, "she groaned, nodded her head and burped. It was one of my greatest scenes – a little weak on dialogue, perhaps, but beautifully staged and not overplayed."[18]

Meanwhile Hitchcock's relationship with star director Cutts had gone sour. Whilst filming *The Prude's Fall* in various places around Europe, Cutts' jealousy of Hitch became evident and he ordered Michael Balcon to fire him from the company. However, Balcon was so impressed with Hitch's work that he instead asked him to direct a film. Hitchcock maintained he was surprised by this development since he had no intention of directing at that time. Balcon sent Hitch to Germany's Emelka studios and on location around Europe to direct *The Pleasure Garden* (1925). It proved to be a baptism by fire.

Alfred J. Hitchcock (1925)
An early version of the most famous profile in the world.

ABOVE
Still from 'The Pleasure Garden' (1925)
Patsy (Virginia Valli) and Levett (Miles Mander)
enjoy their honeymoon at Lake Como. The
filming was not as placid as the onscreen action.

RIGHT
Still from 'The Pleasure Garden' (1925)
Jill (Carmelita Geraghty) is a girl looking for a
good time, especially with Russian princes
(C. Falkenburg).

Hitchcock left Munich railway station on Saturday, 6 June 1925, with actor Miles Mander, cameraman Baron Giovanni Ventimiglia, an actress to play the native girl, a newsreel cameraman, a camera and 10,000 feet of film. Ventimiglia told Hitch not to declare the film or the camera (hidden under Hitch's berth) when they crossed the border into Austria so that the studio would save money on duty. The film was discovered and confiscated. Hitch arrived in Genoa, Italy, on Sunday without film but having to shoot the departure of an ocean liner at midday Tuesday. On Monday the newsreel cameraman was dispatched to Milan to buy film stock from Kodak, but then the confiscated film arrived and they had to pay the duty. Spending all his time converting German Deutschmarks into English Pounds then into Italian Lire, Hitch commented, "I spent more time doing the accounts than I did directing the picture."[19] Somebody saw Hitch counting 10,000 lire and stole it from him, so Hitch had to borrow money from his leading man and cameraman to pay the hotel expenses.

The film focuses on chorus girl Patsy Brand (top American star Virginia Valli) who marries Levett (Miles Mander), a soldier of fortune who goes to the English colonies in the Tropics. She sees her best friend Jill corrupted by the seedy nightlife and become a loose woman. When Patsy finds out Levett is ill, she goes to him only to find Levett an alcoholic living with a native girl. Levett drowns the girl then tries to kill Patsy. A local doctor shoots Levett and Jill's jilted fiancé gets Patsy.

In San Remo, as they were about to film the scene where Levett drowns the native girl, Hitch noticed that Ventimiglia, Mander and the girl were in conference. Mander had to break it to Hitch that the girl couldn't go into the water because of her period. The 25-year-old Hitch didn't know what that was and it had to be explained to him. The actress was shipped back to Munich and her double was able to drown successfully. However, she was somewhat larger and consequently Mander found it difficult to pick her up and carry her out of the water, to the amusement of the gathering crowd. When Mander did eventually manage it, an old lady walked into the shot and looked straight at the camera.

Alma Reville met up with the production at Lake Como, bringing Virginia Valli and Carmelita Geraghty, American actresses who were accustomed to the best of everything, much to Hitch's chagrin. Not only was Carmelita Geraghty not accounted for in the tight budget but they both brought mountains of luggage which incurred additional fees. Also, instead of staying at a moderate hotel they insisted on the Hotel Claridge and the best of everything. Hitchcock got an advance on his fee from Balcon to pay for some of these expenses, but the bulk of the cost was met by Alma's secret loan from Virginia Valli. What Alma said to get this substantial sum has never been revealed. Returning to Munich by train, Hitchcock persuaded the Americans that the train's restaurant was awful, so they ate sandwiches in their compartment. The money saved was just enough to pay for a meal for the rest of the crew.

The remainder of the film was shot without undue incident at Emelka Studios in Munich, where Hitch was more comfortable and had control of his environment. After Alma edited it together, Michael Balcon visited to look at the finished film. He was so impressed that he immediately offered Hitch another film to be shot in Germany. *The Mountain Eagle* (1926) is a rather implausible melodrama about jealousy in a mountain village. Filmed on location in the Austrian Tyrol and

On the set of 'The Mountain Eagle' (1926)
Alma Reville attends to the grooming of German actor Bernhard Goetzke.

Still from 'The Mountain Eagle' (1926)
This feud drama features sexual harassment, corruption, wrongful imprisonment, shooting and strangling. No print of the film is known to exist.

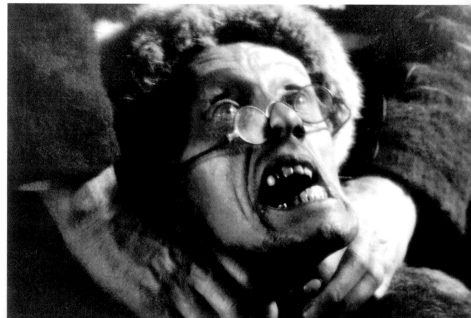

Still from 'The Mountain Eagle' (1926)
Fear o' God Fulton (Malcolm Keen) races across the mountains to save his sick baby.

at Emelka Studios, it featured the extraordinary presence of Bernhard Goetzke, the giant who had played in Fritz Lang's *Der Müde Tod* (*Destiny*, 1921) and *Dr Mabuse der Spieler* (*Dr Mabuse the Gambler*, 1922). Here he is Pettigrew, a Justice of the Peace who is enraged when schoolmistress Beatrice Talbot rejects his advances. He accuses her of seducing his crippled son and she is driven out of the community into the mountains where she meets and marries hermit John Fulton. Fulton and Pettigrew had been rivals for a women before – Pettigrew won her hand in marriage but still the bitterness continues. Eventually, after Fulton is jailed then released for a crime he did not commit, he and Beatrice settle down to a loving relationship.

Hitchcock and Alma returned to London in January 1926, having completed work on both films. Whilst Alma continued to edit scripts and film in Islington, Hitch became increasingly frustrated when first *The Pleasure Garden* and then *The Mountain Eagle* were viewed and shelved by the distributors. C.M. Woolf of the distribution company thought that Hitchcock's weird angles and strange

ABOVE
Publicity still for 'The Lodger' (1926)
Hitchcock said that he was not a Catholic artist
but he often used the iconography, as can be
seen in this image of the lodger (Ivor Novello).

RIGHT
Still from 'The Lodger' (1926)
The lodger enters the house. His exaggerated but
precise stance is calculated to create a creepy
aura around the character.

*"The Lodger is the first picture possibly influenced
by my period in Germany. The whole approach to
the film was instinctive with me. It was the first
time I exercised my style. In truth, you might also
say that The Lodger was my first picture."*

Alfred Hitchcock[24]

Germanic lighting would not be understood by an English audience. Michael
Balcon still had confidence in Hitch and in late April offered him *The Lodger*,
based on the best-selling novel by Marie Belloc Lowndes. Hitch snapped up
the offer and worked with playwright Eliot Stannard to produce a script whilst
simultaneously drawing up production designs. They wrote at such speed that
production began in the first week of May.

This thriller, loosely based on the Jack the Ripper murders, tells of a mysterious stranger (Ivor Novello) who takes rooms in the house of the Bunting family.
They are suspicious of him because he goes out every Tuesday night, which is
when The Avenger claims his next blonde victim. Despite these suspicions, Daisy
Bunting falls for the beautiful young man, much to the consternation of her
boyfriend Joe Betts, a Scotland Yard detective. More out of jealousy than suspicion, Joe has the lodger arrested. The lodger escapes with Daisy, is chased by a
manic lynch mob and is almost killed by them before they find out that the real
killer has been caught.

The ending indicates Hitch's first brush with the star system. Although it was
clear from Lowndes' novel that the lodger was the murderer, it was commercially
impossible for Ivor Novello, then Britain's biggest box-office draw, to play a killer,
so the ending had to be changed. However, Hitchcock adds a final touch. The
flashing neon sign 'To-Night Golden Curls' is shown throughout the movie as a
sign of the constant presence of The Avenger. At the end, although the Avenger
is imprisoned and the hero and heroine kiss in the bright light, the neon sign
still flashes in the black night behind them. Hitchcock's inclusion of the sign is
ambiguous. It could mean that the lodger and Daisy will consummate their relationship, or that perhaps there are other Avengers at large ready to claim more
blonde victims.

The film contains many sinuous camera shots as Hitchcock carefully moved
the camera around the sets as he had seen the Germans do. Famously, there is a
shot looking directly down a stairwell, and all we see is a hand holding the rail,
circling as the lodger descends the stairs. Climbing and descending stairs was a

LEFT
Still from 'The Lodger' (1926)
The lodger's hands are handcuffed and he hangs from the railing at the mercy of the lynch mob. Handcuffs and hanging reoccur in many of Hitchcock's films.

BELOW
Still from 'The Lodger' (1926)
Trick shots often had to be used in the silent cinema to substitute for sound. Here the Bunting family look up at their ceiling and hear the lodger pacing up and down. To show this, Hitchcock made a glass ceiling.

favourite recurring motifs for Hitchcock. For example, Cary Grant carrying the glass of milk in *Suspicion* (see page 91), or James Stewart climbing the stairs in *Vertigo* (see page 154). In fact, the very first image in *The Pleasure Garden* is of chorines descending a spiral staircase.

Another, more instantly recognisable motif was Hitchcock himself. *The Lodger* was the first film in which he made a cameo appearance. Hitch said he needed somebody to fill the foreground space in a newsroom so he filled it. Later, wearing a cap, he can be seen leaning against the railings when the lodger is rescued from the lynch mob. Hitch always maintained that his cameo roles were a bit of fun at first and then became a superstition. Later, when the general public spent too much time looking for the cameo, he got them over with as soon as possible. (For a full list of cameo appearances see page 130.)

The most subtle storytelling device in the film is Hitchcock's presentation of the mysterious lodger. In the first half of the movie, he is dressed in black and placed in shadows, so that we don't empathise with him. After the second murder, when the Buntings suspect that he is The Avenger, Hitchcock bathes him in light and he is dressed in bright clothes so that we subconsciously like him. This manipulation of audience identification through visual presentation was a trademark that Hitchcock used throughout his career.

As 1926 drew to a close, Hitchcock did not have a career to look forward to. He had completed three films but none of them had been released. C.M. Woolf also considered *The Lodger* unsuitable for an audience and shelved it. Regardless, Hitchcock and Alma married on 2 December 1926, cementing a partnership that would endure for the rest of their days. It was a working as well as a private relationship. It is not generally acknowledged that Alma was Hitchcock's greatest collaborator. One day older than him, Alma had begun work in movies at the age of 16, working as an actress, continuity girl and editor long before Hitchcock had written his first title-card. She was credited on many of his films, from Hitchcock's first in 1925 up until *Stage Fright* in 1950, but she had far more of an impact than those credits suggest. Each day, when Hitchcock

ABOVE
2 December 1926
Alfred and Alma get married.

RIGHT
153 Cromwell Road, London (circa 1930)
Alfred discusses a production with Alma, whilst an assistant takes notes.

returned home, he would discuss the day's script with her and together they would tighten it, then create new visual and verbal ideas for the next day's session with whichever world-famous writer he was employing at the time.

The first fruit of their collaboration, *The Pleasure Garden*, was released on 24 January 1927 to acclaim, with the *Daily Express* critic calling Hitchcock 'a young man with a master mind.' Three weeks later *The Lodger* was released to even greater acclaim and there were long queues of people anxious to see the latest film from the boy genius. *The Mountain Eagle* was released in May, but it failed to capture anybody's imagination. Even today it is difficult to judge the merits of the film because no prints are known to exist. Only thirty stills are extant as well as contemporaneous reviews. Hitchcock considered its non-existence no great loss to the world.

By the end of 1927 Hitchcock had filmed and released three further features. The resultant publicity of these six films forever imprinted the name Alfred Hitchcock on the minds of the British film-going public. So much so that when film distributors conducted surveys about the industry, Alfred Hitchcock was virtually the only British director the public could name, and he was named in the thousands, whilst others were listed in single figures. Hitchcock had asserted right from the beginning that "the name of the director should stay clearly in the mind of the audiences" and he had proved himself correct.

Still from 'Downhill' (1927)
From the beginning of his career, Hitchcock constructed detailed sets and lit them beautifully. This is a house in Marseilles.

The German Expressionist influence on Hitchcock was not just technical or visual. German films of the 1920s often told modern fairy tales about innocent people thrown into the middle of the big, bad, industrial, sexual, corrupt city and their subsequent harrowing emotional adventures. In many cases, the story ended badly for the moral characters who were crushed by an amoral world. Although the films sought to depict realism and truth, the storytelling expressed the bewildered and frightened point of view of the central characters using unusual cinematic devices. Virtually all of Hitchcock's movies follow this blueprint, whether he was directing thrillers or comedies or horror films. However, before he was known for his thrillers and became the 'Master of Suspense', Hitchcock applied this blueprint to melodramas, where the status quo must be re-established at the end of the story.

Downhill (1927), co-written by and starring Ivor Novello, follows Roddy, the first son of the rich Berwick family, who is expelled from school when he takes the blame for his friend Tim's theft. When his father throws him out,

we see Roddy going down an escalator in the London Underground – a visual bludgeoning of the 'down' motif. This shot had to be filmed after midnight when the Underground had closed so Hitchcock went to the theatre first. At that time people dressed in top hat and tails for the theatre, so Hitchcock arrived on the set impeccably dressed. "The most elegant moment of direction I've ever had," he later told Peter Bogdanovich.[20] The film follows Roddy's downward spiral into alcoholism until the family finds out the truth and Roddy's honour is restored. Although Hitchcock tried to spice it up with dream sequences, it was hampered by the peculiarity of a man in his thirties playing a schoolboy and by not being very good.

Still from 'Downhill' (1927)
After Roddy Berwick (Ivor Novello) is cast out of his home and inheritance, he goes on a voyage of discovery. At one stage an actress (Isabel Jeans) marries him but leaves him when his money runs out.

Easy Virtue (1927) was hampered by a lack of words. Based on the Noel Coward play, it focuses on Larita Filton, a woman who is accused by her husband of being in love with an artist. There is a scandalous divorce case and the artist kills himself. Larita's world is destroyed, so she decides to change her identity and start a new life. She falls in love and marries a rich young man, John Whittaker, but when his mother finds out about Larita's 'easy virtue' she tells her son everything. Larita is divorced again and her life is in shreds.

In the scene where John proposes to Larita, she tells him to telephone later for a reply. The call and the reply are expressed through the telephone operator who listens in on the conversation – her facial expressions convey the hope, disappointment and eventual delight of John before the operator happily returns to her romantic novel. Again, Hitchcock found a way to tell the story in an oblique but efficient manner. It was these little touches that Hitchcock liked to invent and play with and he found plenty of opportunity to include them in The Ring (1927), a film he wrote as well as directed.

The Ring is about a love triangle between One Round Jack, who takes on allcomers in a travelling carnival, his fiancée Mabel and the Australian boxing champion, Bob Corby. Without revealing who he is, Bob challenges and beats Jack.

ABOVE
Still from 'Easy Virtue' (1927)
Many of Hitchcock's films focus on the romantic complications of the central characters. Larita Filton (Isabel Jeans) is rejected by her husband's family because of her 'notorious' past, rather like Melanie in 'The Birds'.

OPPOSITE
Still from 'Easy Virtue' (1927)
Hitchcock's voyeuristic camera shows the audience secrets. Here the characters are framed in the doorway to make the audience feel they are looking through a keyhole.

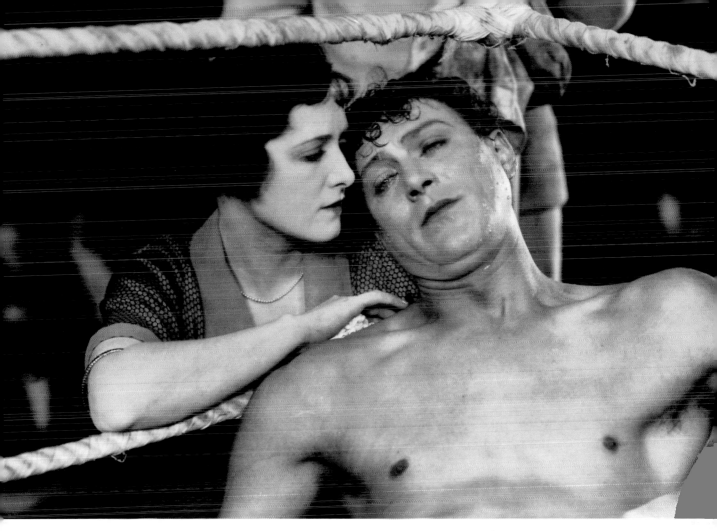

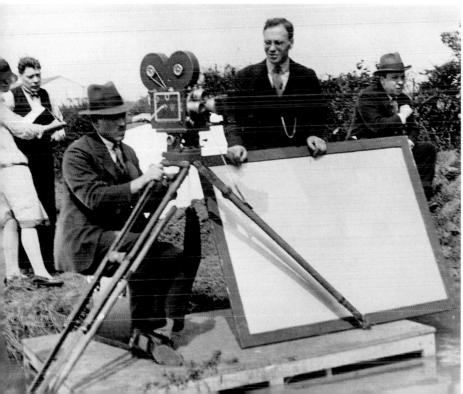

ABOVE
Still from 'The Ring' (1927)
One Round Jack (Carl Brisson) and Bob Corby
literally fight for the love of Mabel (Lilian Hall-
Davis)

LEFT
On the set of 'The Ring' (1927)
Jack Cox sits behind the hand-cranked Mitchell
camera. On the first day of shooting he was
working with a camera and director that were
both new to him, and he was asked to film a
montage of eight dissolves. The success of that
footage began a long and fruitful relationship
with Alfred Hitchcock (right).

OPPOSITE
Still from 'The Ring' (1927)
One Round Jack takes on all comers, assisted
by characters played by Gordon Harker and
Harry Terry.

Still from 'The Farmer's Wife' (1927)
Seeing his daughter married prompts widower Samuel Sweetland (Jameson Thomas) to search for a wife, with hilarious consequences.

"[Film is] the juxtaposition of different pieces of film to create emotion in a person."

Alfred Hitchcock[6]

Then the Australian hires Jack as his sparring partner to be near Mabel. When Bob and Mabel run away together, Jack goes into training so that he can exact his revenge in a boxing match at the Albert Hall.

Hitchcock liked to use visual symbols and in this case he introduced a serpentine bracelet. Bob gives the bracelet to Mabel as a sign of his love for her and Jack later winds it around Mabel's finger like a wedding band. So the ring of the title not only refers to the boxing ring but to the wedding ring that the men are fighting for.

The verve and energy of *The Ring* was followed by the pastoral sweetness of *The Farmer's Wife* (1928), a romantic comedy. After his daughter marries, lonely widower Samuel Sweetland feels he should marry again. With the help of his adoring housekeeper, Araminta Dench, Sweetland draws up a list of four likely candidates but each in turn reject him. In the end Sweetland realises he loves the housekeeper and they all live happily ever after. Although quite static, *The Farmer's Wife* is sumptuously photographed by Hitchcock (Jack Cox was ill for most of the shoot), and has some splendid comic performances in the secondary roles. Hitchcock puts his stamp on the film with a sequence where the passage

Still from 'Champagne' (1928)
In this female version of 'Downhill', Betty (Betty
Balfour) is a spoilt brat whose millionaire father
arranges for her to go without money so that she
must work for a living

of time is shown by the number of times the farmer's underclothes have been
washed. There were plenty of underclothes on display in *Champagne* (1928), a
female variation on *Downhill*. It's a dreadful movie and it was followed by *The
Manxman* (1929), another variation on the love triangle, this time set on the
Isle of Man (although filmed in Cornwall).

To a certain degree life was becoming comfortable for Alma, Alfred and new-
born baby Patricia in their London house at 153 Cromwell Road and at their
country retreat in Shamley Green, but it was clear that the early promise Hitchcock had shown in *The Lodger* was not being fulfilled. Although he had built up
a solid working relationship with photographer Jack Cox and his wife Alma that
had produced technically proficient films, the stories had lacked sparkle. That
was all to change with their next movie, *Blackmail* (1929).

Stills from 'The Manxman' (1928)
In this rematch of 'The Ring', fisherman Pete
Quilliam (Carl Brisson, above leading right) and
lawyer Philip Christian (Malcolm Keen, above
leading left) vie for the affection of Kate Cregeen
(Anny Ondra, right).

Stills from 'The Manxman' (1928)
The stills were by Michael Powell, later an acclaimed film director.

ABOVE
On the set of 'Blackmail' (1929)
Alfred Hitchcock does a sound test with Anny Ondra to prove that her German-Czech accent is not suitable for her role as a Cockney girl.

TOP RIGHT
Still from 'Blackmail' (1929)
Alice White (Anny Ondra) contemplates the murder she has just carried out as the jester in the painting laughs at her. The jester's face is very similar to one in a recently-found still from 'The Mountain Eagle'.

RIGHT
Still from 'Blackmail' (1929)
The artist (Cyril Ritchard) has impure thoughts about Alice as she changes. Hitchcock illustrates this by having a shadow fall over the artist's face that looks like a villain's curly moustache.

Some writers have commented that the introduction of sound killed the pure visual aesthetic of the cinema for many years because the sound had to be recorded live (the dialogue could not be added afterwards) and heavy, noisy cameras could not be moved. However, it should be remembered that sound also added another element that could be used to tell the story and Hitchcock was quick to realise this during the filming of *Blackmail*, one of Britain's first talkies.

Blackmail is about Alice, a blonde virgin who cheats on her boyfriend by going out with an artist. When the artist tries to seduce her, she kills him with a knife then returns home shocked and distraught. Her boyfriend, Frank Webber, who is a police detective at Scotland Yard, finds her glove at the murder scene and hides it out of love for her. A seedy blackmailer, Tracy, has the other glove and tries to profit from it, but Frank frames Tracy for the murder. After an exciting chase through the British Museum, Tracy falls to his death. Alice, racked with guilt, tries to confess to the murder but events contrive to let her go free with her boyfriend. As Alice and Frank leave the police station they do not hold hands or embrace. A distance has entered their relationship and they will never be the same again.

Originally filmed silent (a silent version was released to cinemas that could not afford the expensive sound equipment), at the last minute producer John Maxwell decided to add sound on the last reel of *Blackmail*. Instead, Hitchcock spread the sound throughout the film. This impressed the production company so much that he was allowed to reshoot several key scenes with sound. However, Anny Ondra, who played Alice, had a thick German-Czech accent that would be incongruous in a Cockney London setting, so Hitch had actress Joan Barry say the words into a microphone offstage whilst Anny mimed the words in front of the camera. These solutions illustrated two of Hitchcock's qualities that enabled him to rise within the film community: he knew how to impress producers; and he knew how to solve technical difficulties when making films.

The film is full of dynamic and inventive imagery. In the opening sequence, two cops enter a room and a man is on the bed reading the paper, oblivious to the cops. Then the camera pans from his face to a mirror, then zooms into the mirror, where we can see the faces of the cops. Later, when Alice decides to give herself up, she writes a confession then rises. As she rises, the shadow of a noose falls around her neck. The assured visual style of the film was occasionally marred by static dialogue scenes. However, Hitchcock played with sound in the same way that he played with images. For example, Tracy, the blackmailer has an upper-class accent, quite at odds to his slimy disposition. He was a precursor of the upper-class, avuncular villains that were to haunt the heroes of Hitchcock's future movies. As Frank searches the murder scene he whistles 'Sonny Boy,' a cheeky reference to Al Jolson's hit film *The Singing Fool* of the previous year. The most talked-about sequence of the film is the breakfast the morning after the murder. When Alice is asked to cut the bread (the knife and bread are like the knife and bread beside the dead artist's bed) she picks up the knife whilst a neighbour babbles on about the murder using the word "knife" all the time. The neighbour's words become softer and lower, but the word 'knife' stays loud, so when Alice hears "KNIFE!" the knife jumps out of her hand such is her shock. In a black-comedy touch typical of Hitchcock, her father says, "'Ere! You might've cut someone with that!"

"… all villains are not black and all heroes are not white. There are grays everywhere."

Alfred Hitchcock [4]

Still from 'Blackmail' (1929)
Tracy (Donald Calthrop) enjoys a cigar as he cheerfully blackmails Alice and her boyfriend Frank. He was the first of Hitchcock's upper-class villains.

Still from 'Blackmail' (1929)
The Chief Inspector (Harvey Braban) and
Detective Frank Webber (John Longden) watch
a criminal.

Upon release, *Blackmail* was a phenomenal financial and critical success, the talk of Britain both on radio and in the print media, and Hitchcock found himself inundated with requests for interviews. Instead of engaging a press agent, Hitchcock formed a limited company, Hitchcock Baker Productions, to advertise and promote Alfred Hitchcock, which it did successfully. His past experience with production companies had taught him that they may come and go but he had to look after his own interests and make sure he could always walk into another job. But first he had to fulfil his commitment to British International Pictures and direct the films they chose.

Still from 'Blackmail' (1929)
Alice (Anny Ondra, foreground) has breakfast the morning after killing the artist.

The coming of sound meant that traditional variety hall acts like singers and comedians could now perform on the silver screen. Several successful films of musical and comedy revues had been made in America and British International Pictures wanted to emulate their success in the UK. The result was *Elstree Calling* (1930), Britain's first musical, cobbled together by various different producers and directors. Hitch contributed the framing device (a family trying to watch the show on their television set), a short parody of Shakespeare's *The Taming of the Shrew* and a sketch called 'Thriller.' Apparently, Hitch did not spend more than seven hours on the set.

He spent a little more time on *Juno and the Paycock* (1930), an adaptation of the famed Sean O'Casey play about an Irish family who are told they are to get a big inheritance and are corrupted by the wealth. O'Casey wrote an additional scene, but it's basically a film of the stage play using the original cast of the successful Abbey Theatre production. Hitchcock would later return to the problem of filming a stage play with *Rope* and *Dial M for Murder*.

At a time when bulky sound equipment and noisy machinery kept the camera firmly rooted to a single spot, *Murder!* (1930) proved to be full of cinematic experimentation. One of the opening tracking shots, for example, has the camera move across an immobile crowd looking at the murdered woman on the floor. The camera, slowly, painfully moves from one face/body to the other, eventually following the arm/hand of the murderess to the poker and the dead body. It is a seminal shot that has echoes in the work of Martin Scorsese and David Lynch.

The story seems quite conventional (an actress is convicted of murder and sentenced to hang but one of the jurors, Sir John Menier (Herbert Marshall), tries to prove her innocence by investigating the acting troupe) but Hitchcock adds some interesting touches about gender roles. There are women in male roles (the female barrister and the jury women as experts on psychology), men in female roles (Handel Fane does a trapeze act in drag) and great emphasis on people changing clothes/identities. Although Fane is revealed to have killed so that he is not revealed as a half-caste, his effeminate nature suggests that his real reason was to protect his homosexual identity.

Murder! may have been a failure but at least it had some interesting moments. *The Skin Game* (1931) didn't even have those. A static and stagnant story about two rich families feuding over a piece of land, it seems as though Hitchcock merely arrived at the set, rolled the camera and let the actors speak their lines. Hitch was much more engaged by *Rich and Strange* (1932), perhaps because this black comedy resembled his and Alma's misadventures in Paris on their honeymoon and their 1931 round-the-world trip with their daughter Patricia.

Still from 'Elstree Calling' (1930)
Hitchcock directed a few short sequences, including the linking story, for this variety revue film.

"… with the help of television, murder should be brought into the home where it rightly belongs."

Alfred Hitchcock[25]

LEFT
Still from 'Juno and the Paycock' (1930)
Hitchcock effectively directed a theatre version of
the Sean O'Casey play. He felt restricted because
he could not represent O'Casey's excellent
dialogue in a visual form.

BELOW
On the set of 'Juno and the Paycock' (1930)
Every sound, including the noises in the street
and on the radio, had to be recorded live. As well
as a microphone hanging over the table for the
main performers, there is also one to the left of
the fireplace for the off-camera performers.

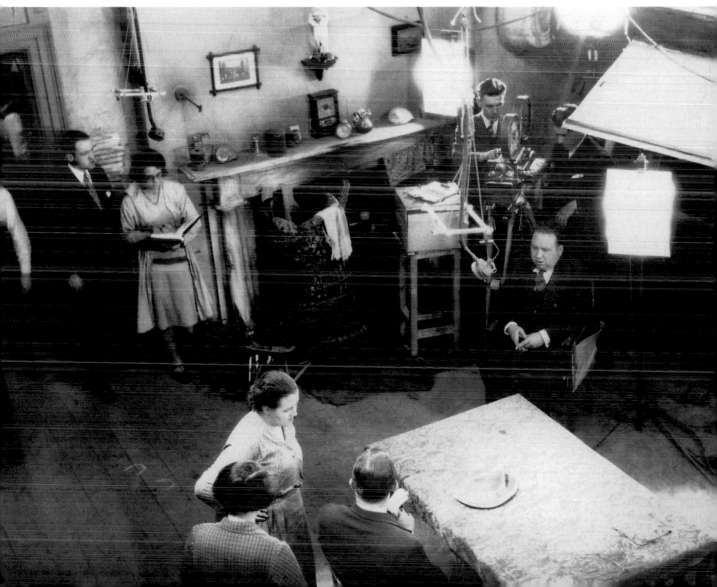

Still from 'Murder!' (1930)
A straightforward murder mystery, it opens with
a tableau of people finding the body (look at it
in the mirror). Hitchcock's slow pan across the
characters has been emulated by Martin
Scorsese and David Lynch amongst others.

Still from 'The Skin Game' (1931)
Chloe (Phyllis Konstam) attempts suicide in this melodramatic clash between two landowners.

On the set of 'Rich and Strange' (1932)
The opening shot of the film is an intricate one, moving from the clock to the men working at their desks and then panning around to the right. Hitchcock is on the camera platform, giving instructions to the men (bottom left) to make sure they pull the camera up the ramp at the correct moment.

In *Rich and Strange*, accountant's clerk Fred Hill (could the name represent Alfred H?) and his wife Emily (Alma?) yearn for an adventurous life rather than their dreary middle-class existence. When they receive a large amount of money from an uncle, they take a luxury trip around the world. They are romanced and their marriage is in tatters but a series of misfortunes brings them together. In the end they return to their dreary London home and start bickering about arrangements for the baby they plan to have. Although they love each other, the couple still have to make compromises to live together.

As in *Downhill*, the characters undergo a rite of passage whilst on a journey, which prefigures the many chases Hitch would choreograph in later films. During the sequence when the tramp steamer is sinking, Hitch remains focused on the couple in their cabin, the water rising in the porthole and seeping under the door, gunshots and shouting penetrating the walls, giving a fearfully claustrophobic feeling. Hitch later repeated this idea for the plane crash in *Foreign Correspondent*.

The dark humour and bittersweet tone of *Rich and Strange* was not understood and Hitch became despondent as another of his films failed to ignite the box office. The same fate befell *Number Seventeen* (1932), a ludicrous but strangely watchable thriller set in a dark house. The dialogue is crisp and there are many visual and audio touches. For example, when a dead body is discovered, a scream is covered by the screaming whistle of a train going by. The screaming face is reminiscent of the woman shot in the famous Odessa Steps sequence of Sergei Eisenstein's *Battleship Potemkin* (1925). Hitch liked the effect so much he repeated it in *The 39 Steps*.

Since *Elstree Calling*, Hitch had been paid a lot of money as part of his contract with British International Pictures and was contractually bound to direct what they suggested even if he objected to it. Hitchcock was depressed because he had been forced to make pictures he didn't like and then watch them fail miserably. Not only that, his recent track record made him unemployable. At this, his lowest ebb, he directed *Waltzes from Vienna* (1933), a musical about the Strauss family. It was hampered by a lack of music and Hitchcock's abominable behaviour towards the stars, Jessie Matthews and Esmond Knight. Hearing of Hitch's dissatisfaction, Michael Balcon offered him the opportunity to make suspense films again. Hitch was delighted, and so began his most creative period in Britain.

OPPOSITE
Still from 'Rich and Strange' (1932)
After being shipwrecked on their glamorous trip around the world, Emily (Joan Barry) and Fred Hill (Henry Kendall) are so hungry they eat a cat.

PAGES 54/55
On the set of 'Rich and Strange' (1932)
Lights and mirrors help marry the model (left) with the street set. Hitchcock stands at the end of the pavement with his hands on his hips.

RIGHT
Still from 'Number Seventeen' (1932)
Allardyce (John Stuart) and Sheldrake (Garry Marsh) in a close-up dirty fight. Hitchcock featured many such fights over the course of his career.

BELOW
On the set of 'Number Seventeen' (1932)
Hitchcock (sitting by the camera) introduces his daughter Patricia to the intricacies of film-making.

LEFT
Publicity still from 'Waltzes from Vienna' (1933)
Jessie Matthews, England's most popular
musical star at the time, played Rasi. Hitchcock
made her life a misery during the production
by making sarcastic jokes and interrupting
her rehearsals. It was generally felt by the cast
and crew that Hitchcock did not know what
he was doing. This was confirmed one hot
afternoon when Hitchcock stood up in front of
the production and announced: "I hate this sort
of stuff. Melodrama is the only thing I can do."

BELOW
Still from 'Waltzes from Vienna' (1933)
Johann Strauss (Esmond Knight) tries to get the
attention of his sweetheart Rasi.

Still from 'The Man Who Knew Too Much' (1934)
Jill Lawrence (Edna Best) gestures at her husband. The comedy of the opening sequences makes the murder of Louis Bernard even more shocking.

In retrospect, it is easy to see that *The Man Who Knew Too Much* (1934) contained the seeds from which many of Hitchcock's subsequent thrillers would germinate. Jill and Bob Lawrence are in St Moritz for Jill to take part in a shooting competition, when they witness the assassination of their friend Louis from whom they receive a secret message. Before they tell the authorities, spies kidnap their daughter Betty to ensure the family's silence. Back in London, Bob tracks down the anarchist group, led by Abbott, while Jill stops an assassination attempt at the Albert Hall. There follows an extended gun battle between the anarchists and the police that is reminiscent of the celebrated 1911 Siege of Sidney Street. The climax sees Jill shoot Ramon (the man who beat her in the shooting competition) when he attacks Betty on a rooftop. Although there are many interesting touches, e.g. Peter Lorre in his first role in English as Abbott is a cultured and likeable villain, the film does not flow and seems forced. However, contemporary audiences were wowed by it and for many years the film had a higher reputation than it deserved.

ABOVE
On the set of 'The Man Who Knew Too Much'
(1934)
Leslie Banks and Peter Lorre act on a not-too-
convincing set representing St Moritz. Hitchcock
is on the far right.

LEFT
Still from 'The Man Who Knew Too Much' (1934)
Bob Lawrence (Leslie Banks) and his daughter
Betty (Nova Pilbeam) with their friend Louis
Bernard (Pierre Fresnay).

RIGHT
Still from 'The Man Who Knew Too Much' (1934)
Abbott (Peter Lorre, centre), the leader of the
anarchists, can be a charming fellow at times.

BELOW
Still from 'The Man Who Knew Too Much' (1934)
The shoot-out is a recreation of the bloody 1911
Siege of Sidney Street where many people lost
their lives.

OPPOSITE
Still from 'The Man Who Knew Too Much' (1934)
Betty temporarily escapes her kidnappers but is
trapped on a roof.

On the set of 'The 39 Steps' (1935)
Hitchcock directing the handcuffed Madeleine
Carroll and Robert Donat on the first day of
filming.

Hitchcock and his collaborators then ironed out all the plot, motivation, dialogue and rhythm problems to make Hitchcock's first masterpiece, *The 39 Steps* (1935). It is built around the double chase idea that a man is wrongfully accused of a murder and is chased by the police. He, in turn, has to find the real murderer before the police catch him. In this case, the man is Richard Hannay and, on his adventures from London to Scotland and back, he meets up with a wide cross-section of people, who betray or trust him depending upon their prejudices and assumptions. A milkman doesn't believe that spies are after Hannay, but he understands the idea of Hannay having an illicit affair and wanting to dodge the husband and brother, so he helps Hannay. A crofter only takes Hannay in for money and then turns him in for the reward when the police arrive. A Sheriff arrests Hannay because he trusts the villain, a respected local man.

The love story woven into the chase first shows Pamela's betrayal of Hannay (after he kisses her on the train to hide his face she tells the police "This is the man you want") and later, when they are handcuffed together, she eventually comes to trust him. The handcuffs play a part in one of the sexiest moments in any of Hitchcock's films. Forced to stay the night at a pub, Pamela needs to take off her wet stockings. As she peels them, the back of Hannay's limp hand brushes against her legs. When the spies have been captured at the end of the film, the closing image is of Hannay and Pamela holding hands, the unlocked handcuffs dangling from Hannay's wrist.

If the romantic ending is the purpose of the movie, then the mysterious organisation (The 39 Steps) and the object they want (the plans of a silent aeroplane engine) are merely devices around which the plot revolves. The thing that everybody wants is called the MacGuffin, a name coined by Angus MacPhail, and Hitchcock used a MacGuffin for many of his films. In *Foreign Correspondent* it was Clause 27, in *Notorious* it was uranium ore, in *North by Northwest* it was microfilm in a statue and in *Torn Curtain* It was a formula in Professor Lindt's

LEFT
Production sketch for 'The 39 Steps' (1935)
This sketch by Hitchcock conveys the brooding atmosphere that he wanted to capture for his adaptation of John Buchan's novel.

BELOW
Still from 'The 39 Steps' (1935)
Richard Hannay (Robert Donat) threatens Pamela (Madeleine Carroll).

ABOVE
Still from 'The 39 Steps' (1935)
The lingerie salesmen (Gus McNaugthon and
Jerry Verno) display their wares. 'The 39 Steps'
works because the wit of the dialogue matches
the visual wit.

RIGHT
Production sketch for 'The 39 Steps' (1935)
This sketch, drawn by Hitchcock to help him
visualise the scene before the set was built,
shows Hannay trying to evade capture on the
Scottish Moors.

Still from 'The 39 Steps' (1935)
As with many of Hitchcock's films, the romance of the main characters is the whole point of the story. Although Hannay and Pamela are forced to be together, Hannay meets couples along the way that reflect the different levels of trust in a relationship.

LEFT
Still from 'The 39 Steps' (1935)
This scene shows how closely Hitchcock followed the sketch.

ABOVE
Still from 'Secret Agent' (1936)
Richard Ashenden (John Gielgud) and 'the General' (Peter Lorre) are spies on a mission to find and kill a German agent. Instead they kill an innocent man.

RIGHT
Still from 'Secret Agent' (1936)
Elsa Carrington (Madeleine Carroll), Richard Ashenden and 'the General' recover after a train wreck kills the charming German agent Robert Marvin (Robert Young, background).

head. As Hitchcock explained it, the MacGuffin is important to the characters but not to the audience.

The sparkling script, engaging characters and razor-sharp editing make *The 39 Steps* as enjoyable today as when it was first shown over 60 years ago. However, despite all the books written about and success and praise for Hitchcock's films there are many who do not like Hitchcock's work. Although novelist Graham Greene agrees that Hitchcock 'has always known exactly the right place to put his camera (and there is only one right place in any scene),'[21] he thought that as a writer and producer Hitchcock displayed an 'inadequate sense of reality.'[22] This is to say that story logic and continuity were subservient to the directorial titillations Hitchcock achieves with his camera and editing.

Greene, reviewing *Secret Agent* (1936), wrote that Hitchcock's films 'consist of a series of small 'amusing' melodramatic situations... Very perfunctorily he builds up these tricky situations (paying no attention on the way to inconsistencies, loose ends, psychological absurdities) and then drops them: they mean nothing: they lead to nothing.'[23] This is certainly true of some of Hitchcock's movies and often his successful films are those that closely follow the psychological development of his characters, as in the case of *Notorious*, *The Wrong Man* and *Vertigo*.

In contrast to the high-speed chase of *The 39 Steps*, *Secret Agent* is a sombre and discordant story about a man on a mission to kill a German spy. Based on W. Somerset Maugham's *Ashenden* short stories, John Gielgud is the distant and ambiguous central character around whom the other, more interesting, characters revolve: Peter Lorre is Gielgud's effeminate sidekick, in a role that anticipates his Joel Cairo in *The Maltese Falcon* (1941); Robert Young is cast against type as the charming villain; Madeleine Carroll seems groomed for international stardom. None of these characters connect with each other and when Gielgud kills an innocent man the story does not know where to go, despite Hitchcock's inventive use of sound and images.

ABOVE
Still from 'Secret Agent' (1936)
Elsa Carrington clambers from the climatic train wreck. She changes her moral position on spying over the course of the story. At first she saw killing as her duty, but after they killed an innocent man she holds Ashenden and 'the General' at gunpoint to prevent them killing.

PAGES 68/69
On the set of 'Secret Agent' (1936)
Hitchcock films the aftermath of the train wreck.

ABOVE
Still from 'Sabotage' (1936)
Disturbed by the death of her brother Stevie
through the actions of her husband (Oscar
Homolka), Winnie Verloc (Sylvia Sidney)
subconsciously contemplates murdering him.

OPPOSITE
On the set of 'Sabotage' (1936)
The Verlocs own a cinema, which allowed
Hitchcock to use the films on the screen as
a counterpoint to the human drama.

Hitchcock also killed an innocent in *Sabotage* (1936), a very loose adaptation
of Joseph Conrad's novel *The Secret Agent*. Karl Anton Verloc is a cinema owner
who is paid to sabotage London's power supply. His first effort in London is
greeted with laughter rather than panic, so he is ordered to plant a bomb at Piccadilly Circus during the Lord Mayor's Show. Delayed by Ted, a policeman dis-
guised as a greengrocer, he sends his wife's schoolboy brother Stevie in his stead
who, unaware of the bomb, is killed when it explodes. Verloc's American wife
Winnie finds out Stevie is dead and confronts Verloc. Throughout this stunning
sequence she is silent and we only see the pain in her face as she reacts to Verloc's
words. When the knife in her hand goes (unseen) into Verloc we are unsure if it is
an accident, or if Winnie intended it, or if Verloc thrust himself on it. Winnie is
not charged with murder and the implication, as in *Blackmail*, is that she and Ted
will have an uneasy relationship in the future.

ABOVE
On the set of 'Sabotage' (1936)
It was cheaper to build a set for one shot rather than actually go to London and film during the confusion of the Lord Mayor's Show.

RIGHT
Still from 'Sabotage' (1936)
The finished shot is very convincing. Stevie (Desmond Tester) travels across London unaware that he is carrying a ticking bomb.

On the set of 'Sabotage' (1936)
Another subtle film-making trick. When filming
an insert for the sequence on the opposite page,
Hitchcock only needs two dozen people to create
the effect of thousands. Hitchcock is at bottom
right.

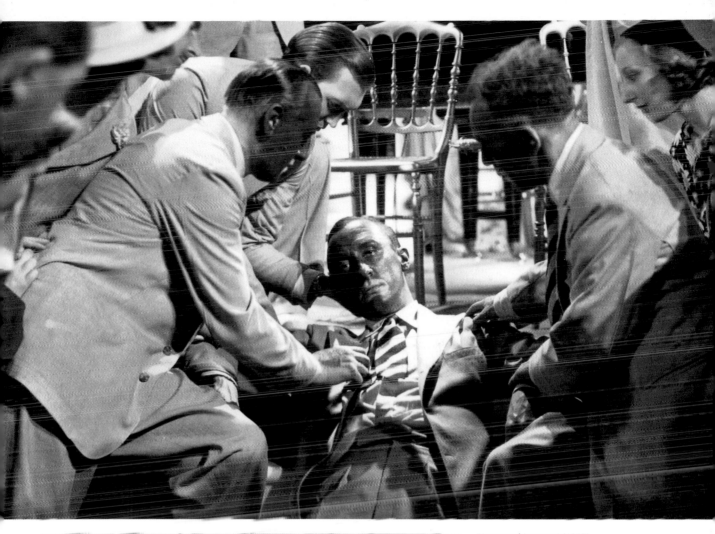

'Young and Innocent' (1937)
One of the most stunning shots in Hitchcock's career is the crane shot high over a hotel lobby, over a ballroom and then down to the dance band into a close-up of the drummer's eyes. His eyes begin to blink, telling the audience that this is the man the young heroes are looking for.

LEFT
Production sketch for 'Young and Innocent' (1937)
The ballroom.

OPPOSITE
On the set of 'Young and Innocent' (1937)
It took two days of rehearsals before the 145 foot shot was perfected. The camera operator had to constantly refocus as the camera moved, eventually stopping just 4 inches from the drummer's face.

ABOVE
Still from 'Young and Innocent' (1937)
Frightened that he will be found out, the drummer collapses, thus drawing attention to himself.

There was little opportunity for such visual flamboyance in *The Lady Vanishes* (1938), the story of an old lady who vanishes from a moving train. Working from a fantastic script by Frank Launder and Sidney Gilliat, this soufflé of English caricatures abroad becoming embroiled in espionage is lightweight but tasty. There are many subtle touches in the script that are easy to overlook. For example, although Iris searches for the missing Miss Froy, over the course of the adventure it is the haughty lady inside Iris that vanishes and her true, romantic character that emerges.

ABOVE
Still from 'The Lady Vanishes' (1938)
In the climatic shoot-out, the English travellers are trapped in the restaurant carriage at teatime.

OPPOSITE
On the set of 'The Lady Vanishes' (1938)
This fabulous adventure was filmed on an 80-foot-long studio in five weeks.

ABOVE
Still from 'Jamaica Inn' (1939)
Sir Humphrey Pengallan (Charles Laughton, centre) is a Cornish magistrate who runs a gang of ship wreckers. He holds a gun to Mary Yelland's (Maureen O'Hara) head and is watched by naval officer Jem Treharne (Robert Newton).

OPPOSITE
On the set of 'Jamaica Inn' (1939)
Stuntman Sam Lee practises being hanged in preparation for filming. Hitchcock looks on approvingly.

"You can't direct a [Charles] Laughton picture. The best you can hope for is to referee."

Alfred Hitchcock

Many films were being made in Britain in the late 1930s but they were made inefficiently and the losses incurred led to the closure of several studios. Hitchcock realised that the only way he could make a lot of money was to move to America. He canvassed the studios in Hollywood with little success. Only David O. Selznick seemed interested so, after some haggling, Hitch signed a 4-picture deal with him on 14 July 1938 in New York where Hitch would get $40,000 a picture, plus a generous weekly salary when he wasn't filming. Hitch returned to England to quickly film his outstanding commitment, the disappointing historical melodrama *Jamaica Inn*, and then moved to America.

"The Kind of a Guy Who Restores Your Faith in This Whole Lousy Business" 1940–1954

Having been trained by American people in an American studio that happened to be in London, it was no surprise that Hitchcock moved to America to work in the Hollywood system. The fact that Hitch needed a job because there was no English film industry only helped to speed up the move. Arriving in New York on 6 March 1939, Hitchcock and his family eventually reached Los Angeles at the end of the month.

Hitch had worked on a script for *Rebecca*, based on Daphne du Maurier's best-selling novel, but David O. Selznick rejected it in a typically long and cogent memo. Selznick, three years into the production of the film that would make his name, *Gone With the Wind* (1939), was a producer who loved and understood books. He wanted the essence of and, in some cases, precise scenes and dialogue from *Rebecca* to be represented faithfully on screen. His literal approach was in direct contrast to Hitchcock's visualisation of a scene. For example, Selznick preferred to show the speaker in a dialogue scene whereas Hitchcock preferred to show the reactions of the people listening. In Hitchcock's scenes two levels of information, verbal and visual, complement each other and lead to a more intuitive understanding of characters and their motivations. Selznick, for his part, wanted to maintain the overall psychological depth of the characters without cheapening them with visual trickery and inappropriate scenes.

After extensive rewrites of the script and a laborious casting process, filming of *Rebecca* began on 8 September 1939, five days after Britain declared war on Germany and the day before the first preview of *Gone With the Wind*. Much of the success of *Gone With the Wind* would later be attributed to Selznick's attention to detail about every aspect of the production. He hired and fired directors, selected and approved costumes, was omnipresent on the set and kept several secretaries busy around the clock typing his infamously long and detailed memos. Hitchcock, on the other hand, liked to work alone without interference and to be the master of his own film set. Now Selznick was asking him to justify his choices. Selznick was coming up with good ideas and intelligent points that Hitch had to consider carefully. Up until this time, Hitchcock was a good visual director but he lacked the skill to assess a production as a whole while concurrently attending to the fine detail. Although Hitchcock and Selznick conducted a battle of wills over

On the set of 'Shadow of a Doubt' (1943)
Hitchcock gets involved in the actions of the actors.

"Not a bad guy… although not exactly a guy to go camping with."

David O. Selznick

the next eight years, in the end Selznick instilled in Hitchcock the ideas of solid story structure and consistent characterisation. It was also a period when Hitch learned everything he needed to know about producing films within the Hollywood system.

The normal film-making practice was for a director to film 'master' shots, i.e. the whole sequence from beginning to end with the characters moving and speaking as required, and then to film close-ups and other angles. This was a good working method. The sequence was quickly filmed and was 'safe' because the best takes and angles could be selected in the editing process. Certainly Selznick liked this method because he had more control over the film when it came to be edited. Hitchcock did not work this way.

Hitchcock liked to plan his films visually before filming began. This came from his love of German silent cinema, where the story was told with images and without titles to interfere with the rhythm and continuity of a scene. Consequently, the angle and lighting of each piece of film, and the precise way they were edited together, were carefully planned to achieve the required response from the audience. This was a slower way of making a film, but there was no wastage and there was only one way the pieces of film could fit together. This annoyed Selznick because it gave control to Hitchcock, but he was too busy dealing with promotion for *Gone With the Wind* to interfere too much with Hitchcock's working methods on *Rebecca*.

As Bill Krohn points out in *Hitchcock at Work*, although Hitchcock meticulously planned scenes in advance, once he was on the set he spent time rehearsing with the actors. As a result there were often improvisations with the script and Hitchcock's visualisation of it. He even filmed variations on scenes to give different meanings and emphases, then saw how each played in the editing process. The important point here is that Hitchcock did not film the same scene from different angles but that he would film different scenes that might give different outcomes and motivations for the characters.

Rebecca is the story of a timid girl who enters the rich world of her new husband Maxim de Winter and immediately feels out of place. Her insecurity leads her to believe that Rebecca, the first Mrs de Winter, was Maxim's true love and the insidious housekeeper Mrs Danvers encourages this view. The truth is that Rebecca was an evil beauty and that Maxim hated her. This gothic melodrama was perhaps not ideal material for Hitchcock, who was more used to being brutal rather than brooding, but it illustrates themes and practices that came to typify his best work like *Rear Window*, *The Wrong Man*, *Vertigo*, *Psycho* and *The Birds*: the slow, measured pace; taking the point of view of a single character; introducing an element halfway through that completely changes the focus of the story; and only using extraordinary visual devices at key moments of the plot.

The film works because Hitchcock captures Joan Fontaine's central performance as the sweet, gentle, innocent lost soul, and it is the most popular of Hitchcock's films, mainly because of its appeal to women. It received a Best Picture Oscar, collected by Selznick, and cinematographer George Barnes got an Oscar too. Hitchcock was nominated for Best Director, the first of five in his career, but he never won one. More importantly, *Rebecca* established Hitch in America and made him 'hot.' Other producers were now queuing up to pay Selznick for Hitchcock's services.

Production sketch for 'Rebecca' (1940)
A sketch of the eerie Manderley as it was seen at the beginning of the film.

ABOVE
Still from 'Rebecca' (1940)
The second Mrs de Winter (Joan Fontaine)
is encouraged to commit suicide by the
housekeeper Mrs Danvers (Judith Anderson)
who, it is hinted, had unnatural relations with
Rebecca.

PAGES 86/87
On the set of 'Rebecca' (1940)
Alfred Hitchcock and Joan Fontaine chat, with
Hitchcock's assistant Joan Harrison between
them. Joan Harrison went on to produce
Hitchcock's TV series.

ABOVE
Still from 'Foreign Correspondent' (1940)
Diplomat Van Meer is assassinated by a gang
of spies. Or rather, they kill a double to give
themselves time to extract the secret Clause 27
of a peace treaty from the real Van Meer they
have kidnapped.

RIGHT
Still from 'Foreign Correspondent' (1940)
After suave villain Stephen Fisher (Herbert
Marshall, centre) reconciles himself with his
daughter, he throws himself off the wreckage
of a plane crash so that the others can live.

OPPOSITE
Still from 'Foreign Correspondent' (1940)
Reporter Johnny Jones (Joel McCrea, left) follows
the spies to a windmill, where he discovers the
real Van Meer.

nists are not caught by the end of the film and their avuncular leader, Tobin, escapes to the Caribbean until the war blows over.

One of the most intriguing aspects of *Saboteur* is the use of fire and water as recurring motifs. The opening shot is of aircraft plant workers lighting cigarettes on their break, before Fry burns down the plant. Later a policeman advises the captured Kane that he will "have time to burn." As for water, Kane escapes the police by jumping into a river, and later escapes from the fifth columnists by setting off a sprinkler system. Subsequently, Kane averts the destruction of a ship being launched at a Brooklyn shipyard. However, the most symbolic use of these motifs occurs at the end with the flame on the Statue of Liberty, which is surrounded by water. As Fry hides inside the statue, the symbolism is that spies hide under the cloak of liberty.

This underrated film has many fabulous set pieces, including a brilliant scene where Fry runs through a cinema and the dialogue/gunplay on screen ironically matches the 'real-life' situation. "Run, he'll kill you," a screen character shouts and then Fry shoots into the audience in sync with the gunshots on the screen. This wasn't the first time Hitchcock had used the cinema screen in this way. There is a painful scene in *Sabotage* where Winnie, recoiling from the news of her brother's death, retreats into the cinema and hears the song 'Who Killed Cock Robin?' which serves to heighten her grief. These clever visual devices drew attention to Hitchcock the director but he was very adept at more subtle storytelling techniques, as he showed in *Shadow of a Doubt* (1943), one of his favourite films.

As a child Hitch read Victorian literature, like Robert Louis Stevenson's *The Strange Case of Dr Jekyll and Mr Hyde* (1886) and Oscar Wilde's *The Picture of Dorian Gray* (1891), both of which used the idea of good and evil being present within one person. The development of psychoanalysis at the turn of the century and the subsequent recognition of the work of Sigmund Freud and Carl Jung helped people to understand that there can be light and shadow sides to everybody's personality. Hitchcock did not have obviously evil villains with leering grins and black hats. He included cultured and charming villains in many of his films, often showing them with their families or as respected public figures. However, these villains were motivated by lust, greed or ideals. *Shadow of a Doubt* is the first of several films (*Strangers on a Train*, *Psycho* and *Frenzy*) where Hitchcock includes a psychopathic killer.

Shadow of a Doubt begins with Uncle Charlie in Philadelphia and his niece Charlie Newton in Santa Rosa lying on their beds, both thinking that Uncle Charlie should visit Santa Rosa. Corrupt and cynical Uncle Charlie thinks this because he is being pursued by two men through the decaying city. Sweet and innocent Charlie is bored with life in her idyllic small town and complains that nothing ever happens. This duality is re-enforced throughout the film with each scene having its complement: Charlie and Uncle Charlie meet twice at the Till Two diner, and so on. Eventually Charlie discovers that Uncle Charlie is the Merry Widow killer, who strangles his victims, thinking he does the world a favour by disposing of these foul and dirty carrion. This new knowledge about the evil in the world (and by extension, the possibility that she could become evil) is gained concurrently with her growth from childhood into womanhood and her consequent understanding of sexuality and responsibility.

OPPOSITE TOP
On the set of 'Saboteur' (1942)
Hitchcock explains what he wants inside the head of the Statue of Liberty for the climatic sequence. Notice how little of the head is built. This is because Hitchcock often planned the shots he wanted in advance.

OPPOSITE BOTTOM LEFT
Still from 'Saboteur' (1942)
Saboteur Frank Fry (Norman Lloyd) holds a gun on Barry Kane (Robert Cummings, second right) just after Kane prevents a ship from being blown up during its launch.

OPPOSITE BOTTOM RIGHT
Still from 'Saboteur' (1942)
Barry Kane menaces Patricia Martin (Priscilla Lane) who, like Pamela in 'The 39 Steps', initially doubts the innocence of the man on the run but comes to love him.

Location scouting for 'Shadow of a Doubt' (1943)
Playright Thornton Wilder and Alfred Hitchcock
visited Santa Rosa when writing the script so that
they could accurately use the locations and
people. Here they are at the town square.

Location scouting for 'Shadow of a Doubt' (1943)
Hitchcock discusses the security arrangements of the local jail with the sheriff.

On the set of 'Shadow of a Doubt' (1943)
Henry Travers and Hume Cronyn wait at the steps of the house while Hitchcock helps line up the camera. Hitchcock's vision was so precise that he meticulously planned shots to hide and reveal elements on the screen. In this case, the plank is to raise the actors as they walk and talk about the Merry Widow murders. Their bodies will block out Joseph Cotten and Teresa Wright as he realises that she knows he is the murderer they are talking about.

Still from 'Shadow of a Doubt' (1943)
Nice Uncle Charlie Oakley (Joseph Cotten) arrives from Philadelphia to visit his sister Emma Newton (Patricia Collinge) and her family in Santa Rosa, California. He is a charming man but he hides a secret.

The story is all the more chilling because it is set in a family atmosphere, and in a sedate, idyllic small town environment. For his first film with an authentic American background, Hitch asked playwright Thornton Wilder (*Our Town*) to provide the script and then asked author Sally Benson (*Meet Me in St. Louis*) to add family touches. In the end, Hitchcock added many personal touches that made the film his most autobiographical. Hitch had received news that his mother was ill in London but he was obviously unable to travel to be at her side. His mind awash with nostalgia and reminiscences, the normally reticent Hitchcock began to talk to people about his days in Leytonstone and, as Donald Spoto noted in *The Dark Side of Genius*, littered the script with personal references: Charlie's mother is named Emma, like Hitch's mother; Uncle Charlie's childhood bike accident happened to Hitch; Herbie is mother-dominated and obsessed with murder, like Hitch; Ann reads *Ivanhoe*, a book Hitch knew by heart as a child; Joseph (Hitchcock's second name) refuses to drive a car, like Hitch… Whatever the sources, the result is one of Hitchcock's finest films.

Publicity still for 'Shadow of a Doubt' (1943)
Uncle Charlie is really the Merry Widow killer,
a psychopath who strangles his victims. His
niece Charlie Newton (Teresa Wright) suspects
something is wrong and so has to be stopped.

RIGHT
On the set of 'Shadow of a Doubt' (1943)
A part of the house was built in a studio to film
Uncle Charlie's attempt to murder Charlie on
the steps.

PAGE 102 TOP LEFT
Still from 'Lifeboat' (1944)
After a freighter is sunk by a German U-boat
in the mid-Atlantic, the survivors try to scramble
to safety.

PAGE 102 TOP RIGHT
Still from 'Lifeboat' (1944)
Each character on the boat represents a different
type of person. By pitting them against a German
this intelligent propaganda film not only shows
their attitude to war but also their attitude to life.

PAGE 102 BOTTOM
Still from 'Lifeboat' (1944)
The German Willy (Walter Slezak, left) is
confident, strong, intelligent, cunning and a
natural leader. The others on the boat let him
row and take control of their destiny.

PAGE 103
Still from 'Lifeboat' (1944)
The movie was filmed on one set but it retains
visual and emotional interest throughout.

TOP
Still from 'Bon Voyage' (1944)

ABOVE
Still from 'Aventure Malgache' (1944)

OPPOSITE
Still from 'Spellbound' (1945)
Dr Edwardes/JB/John Ballantine (Gregory Peck)
is a disturbed young man who is somehow
involved in murder. His doctor and lover Dr
Constance Peterson (Ingrid Bergman) is trying
to unravel his strange dream.

Hitchcock's first overtly political film was *Lifeboat* (1944), the story of a diverse group of people who survive a U-boat attack and have to make it to Bermuda with no compass. Each of the characters loses the thing they love and the film explores what people are made of when they are stripped bare. A German, who has confidence, energy and a sense of purpose, takes over the boat by sheer force of will. In the end the others join forces to kill the German, but what they have done is a horrible thing. As Constance Porter says, "The sins you do two by two, you pay for one by one."

Lifeboat may have been propaganda, but it was great propaganda. The same cannot be said for the short films *Bon Voyage* (1944) and *Aventure Malgache* (1944), which Hitchcock directed in England for the Ministry of Information with limited resources. They were made to show the newly-liberated France the important role played by the Resistance during the war. In fact *Aventure Malgache* was not even shown in France because it was deemed too politically sensitive. Hitchcock was also a consultant for Sergei Nolbandov's uncompleted documentary about the Nazi concentration camps, the footage for which was later released as *Memory of the Camps* (1945).

Upon his return to America, Hitchcock directed the lacklustre *Spellbound* (1945) for producer David O. Selznick. An enormous hit at the time on account of its stars (Ingrid Bergman and Gregory Peck) and its subject matter (psycho-analysis), it fails to deliver any real tension or excitement. The most interesting sequence is the surreal dream designed by Salvador Dalí that is used as a kind of picture puzzle for Ingrid Bergman to unravel the problems inside Gregory Peck's head. Hitchcock used Bergman's screen insecurity to better effect in *Notorious* (1946). She played Alicia Huberman, the alcoholic daughter of a Nazi, who is recruited by secret agent T. R. Devlin to romance and spy on her father's friend Alexander Sebastian in Rio de Janeiro. Alicia and Devlin are in love (although Devlin will not admit it), yet he asks her to sleep with and marry Sebastian out of duty to her country. In contrast, when Sebastian finds out that Alicia is a spy, he must kill her out of duty, yet helps her escape. Sebastian's love for Alicia seems truer and stronger than Devlin's. It is made all the more tragic when Sebastian is left to die at the hands of his own group after saving Alicia. The moral complexity of the piece, combined with the marvellous performances, make this one of Hitchcock's best films. Film-maker and Hitchcock scholar François Truffaut considered it his favourite black-and-white Hitchcock film.

Whilst developing the script with screenwriter Ben Hecht, Hitchcock was looking for a suitable MacGuffin for the film and decided the spies were smuggling uranium ore so that they could make an atomic bomb. He asked experts who, to lure Hitch away from the truth, said that scientists were using heavy water not uranium ore. Studios even passed on the film because they thought the MacGuffin was too ridiculous. Ironically, Hitchcock had hit upon the real secret ingredient and he later learned that the FBI followed him for three months to find out the source of his information.

They say that behind every great man is a greater woman, and that is certainly the impression that Madame Sebastian gives in relation to her son Alexander. She controls his every move and is one of many dominant older women who recur throughout Hitchcock's work: Nurse Agnes in *The Man Who Knew Too Much* (1934); the Baroness in *The Lady Vanishes*; Mrs Danvers in *Rebecca*; Mrs Van

Still from 'Spellbound' (1945)
This part of John Ballantine's dream sequence, featuring Constance turning into a statue, was not used in the final film. It concerned John's fear of marrying Constance rather than the murder that was central to the plot.

LEFT
On the set of 'Spellbound' (1945)
Alfred Hitchcock and Salvador Dali discuss the dream sequence.

OPPOSITE
Publicity still for 'Spellbound' (1945)
Ingrid Bergman is John Ballantine's dream woman.

ABOVE
Still from 'Notorious' (1946)
This moraly complex film hinges on the relationship of spy T. R. Devlin (Cary Grant) and Alicia (Ingrid Bergman), the guilty daughter of a Nazi. He asks Alicia to marry and make love to a Nazi to get information from him. Thus Devlin puts duty above personal considerations.

RIGHT
Still from 'Notorious' (1946)
Lovers and spies Alicia and Devlin discover the uranium ore in champagne bottles.

Sutton in *Saboteur*; Jessie Stevens in *To Catch a Thief*; Lydia Brenner in *The Birds*; Bernice Edgar in *Marnie*; and of course the omnipotent Mrs Bates in *Psycho*. Hitchcock always had strong women behind him and various scholars have identified both his mother and Alma as the sources for the strong women in his films. In the later films these mothers often try to prevent their offspring having relationships with anyone other than themselves. Thus Alexander Sebastian not only has a rival in Devlin, but in his mother too. If Hitchcock identified with Alexander then it may explain why Alexander is such a sympathetic character.

An older man's desire for a younger woman (as in Alexander's love for Alicia) is echoed several times in Hitchcock's next film, *The Paradine Case* (1947). First, the young Mrs Paradine is accused of poisoning her rich, blind, older husband. Then Anthony Keane, the older barrister defending her, falls for Mrs Paradine's ice-cool beauty. Later Keane's wife is pawed by the lecherous Judge Lord Horfield. This motif is never exploited or developed, although it does reappear in Hitchcock's films throughout the 1950s when actors Ray Milland, James Stewart, Henry Fonda and Cary Grant played against Grace Kelly, Vera Miles, Kim Novak and Eva Marie Saint. This could simply have been a result of ageing male stars, coming to the end of their screen careers, being paired with upcoming female stars. Many commentators have pointed to these relationships as evidence that Hitchcock desired his leading ladies. Hitch may, indeed, have desired the actresses but there is no concrete evidence that he did anything about it, other than flirt in a jocular manner and tell risqué jokes to embarrass them. It is more likely that his desires fuelled the erotic content of his films.

There was always an element of eroticism in Hitchcock's films. From the opening moments of his first film, *The Pleasure Garden*, which featured scantily clad dancers, Hitchcock repeatedly showed women in a state of undress, often eroticising them during moments of peril. Alice White is in her underclothes when she stabs the artist in *Blackmail*. Carefree girls jump around in their underclothes at the beginning of *The Lady Vanishes*. Mrs Danvers provocatively shows the see-through nightdress to the second Mrs de Winter in *Rebecca*. As Charlie runs to the library in *Shadow of a Doubt*, light shines through her dress showing her sexuality for the first time. However, Hitchcock reserved the most intimate moments for the long-delayed kiss. In *Rear Window*, Lisa quietly approaches the recumbent, dozing Jeff and kisses him from above in slow motion. In *Vertigo*, there are two cathartic kisses. In the first Scottie kisses Madeleine to show his love for her. In the second, he kisses Judy who he has obsessively dressed to look like his lost love Madeleine. *Notorious* has perhaps his most intimate and erotic kiss, when Devlin and Alicia do not break their embrace as they talk and kiss as they walk around the room. The picture is framed tightly on their heads throughout. What Hitchcock was trying to capture was the moment early in a relationship when lovers cannot bear to be parted. This idea had crystallised in his mind after seeing a couple embrace at Étaples railway station whilst the man urinated against a brick wall. The woman did would let go of his arm, even whilst he peed.

"The length of a film should be directly related to the endurance of the human bladder."

Alfred Hitchcock

PAGES 110–113
On the set of 'Notorious' (1946)
War photographer Robert Capa was in love with
Ingrid Bergman and wanted to be with her. To
get onto the set of 'Notorious' he pretended to be
doing an article for 'Life' magazine. Consequently
we have images of Hitchcock making one of his
most famous shots. The camera swoops down
into the party to a close-up of the stolen key in
Alicia's hand.

On the set of 'The Paradine Case' (1947)
Hitchcock about to disturb Gregory Peck and
Ann Todd at work.

Alfred Hitchcock was not very interested in *The Paradine Case*, as is evident from the lacklustre film that was released. Hitch resented the amount of money David O. Selznick had made hiring Hitchcock out to producers all over Hollywood (Selznick earned as much as Hitchcock on each deal) and since *The Paradine Case* was his last film for Selznick he did not try very hard.

This was the golden age of cinema-going, when 80 million people went to the movies every week. In the seven years that Hitchcock had been in America his reputation inside the Hollywood community had rocketed. He had worked for a variety of producers, solved every problem put in his path with inventive and arresting results on the screen and, most importantly, helped line his producers' pockets. One executive was overheard saying that Hitchcock was "the kind of a guy who restores your faith in this whole lousy business." Selznick, by contrast, had begun that period by releasing the biggest film in the world, *Gone With the Wind*, and finished it trying to recoup money on the incredibly expensive psychosexual western *Duel in the Sun* (1946).

In fairness, Selznick had helped Hitchcock integrate himself into the Hollywood business world, had given him the opportunity to be his own producer and helped him understand the mechanics of coherent story and characterisation. Selznick had also shown him that in Hollywood it was the producer who had control of the final film. The only way Hitchcock could totally control his films was to become a producer, so he formed his own production company, Transatlantic Pictures, with his old friend Sidney Bernstein and started making films the way he wanted them to be made.

TOP RIGHT
Still from 'The Paradine Case' (1947)
Barrister Anthony Keane (Gregory Peck) becomes so infatuated with Mrs Maddalena Anna Paradine (Alida Valli), who is accused of murder, that he is blind to the truth.

TOP LEFT
On the set of 'The Paradine Case' (1947)
Hitchcock expresses his thoughts to Ann Todd and Ethel Barrymore.

ABOVE
Still from 'The Paradine Case' (1947)
Gay Keane (Ann Todd) suffers the unwelcome physical contact of Judge Lord Horfield (Charles Laughton). This old man's lust for a young woman echoes Anthony Keane's for Mrs Paradine.

Hitchcock was a master of film form but after 36 films he needed to challenge the form to retain his interest. He had already filmed *Lifeboat* on a single set, the majority of *The Lady Vanishes* had been shot on a train and most of *Number Seventeen* was set in a dark house. For *Rope*, Hitchcock wanted to tell the story of homosexual killers Brandon and Philip on one set and using one continuous piece of film recording the action in real time. He wanted to trap the viewers in the room and make them go through the same intense emotions as the characters on the screen. There is a certain irony that the master of cinematic technique wanted his audience to have the same experience as going to a play.

In the end the technique used to make *Rope* helped only to strangle the life out of it. The film was further hindered by the ill-defined relationships between the characters. It is obvious to a modern audience that the killers are homosexual lovers who live together, yet the film presents them more as good friends because of censorship requirements. Consequently the bullying attitude of Brandon towards the weaker Philip, who actually did the strangling, does not have a firm emotional base. The film revolves around the idea that these elitist snobs kill because they want to and that the cocktail party that ensued would, according to Brandon, "make our work of art a masterpiece." Attending are the victim's parents and girlfriend, as well as the killers' mentor Rupert Cadell. Rupert, a publisher of intellectual books, explains to the assembled guests that some people are superior to others and should be allowed to kill their inferiors if they so desire. He only realises that he is wrong when he finds out that his prize students are killers. Rupert is morally culpable for the killing and subsequently helps bring his charges to justice.

The movie is filmed in ten-minute takes (the maximum amount of film held in a film camera) and transitions from one take to the other are covered by the people walking into shot filling the screen, but there is actually one definite cut. When Brandon talks about Philip strangling chickens, Philip shouts and then we cut directly to Rupert's face.

In later years Hitchcock referred to the ten-minute take as a stunt, although *Rope* got good notices and made money at the box office. He also used the technique for some sequences of *Under Capricorn* (1949), a gothic story about a rich ex-convict in Australia, his troubled wife and her amorous cousin. In many ways it resembled both *Rebecca* and *Notorious*, with the large mansion, the scheming housekeeper and the slow poisoning of a wife caught between two loves, but this expensive production had a perfunctory script that no amount of sumptuous decor or good performances could save.

Under Capricorn killed Transatlantic Pictures and any future ambition Hitchcock had to run his own production company, although he would produce every subsequent film during his long career. With his professional future at stake, Hitch took on *Stage Fright* (1950), a weak whodunnit set in the world of the theatre. Even the presence of veteran scene-stealers such as Marlene Dietrich and Alastair Sim could not lift the plodding script. Hitchcock had lost his way. Since *Notorious* the relationships in his films had not been vital, the visuals had been uninspired, the editing had been pedestrian and the dialogue had been bland. Each of these issues had to be addressed by Hitchcock in his capacity as producer and director, and this he did on *Strangers on a Train* (1951), which is often referred to as Hitchcock's 'comeback' film.

Still from 'Rope' (1948)
Philip (Farley Granger) and Rupert Cadell (James Stewart) fight when Rupert realises that his two students have killed somebody to prove their superiority.

On the set of 'Rope' (1948)
Farley Granger and John Dall rehearse the
strangulation scene that opens the film.
Hitchcock is visibly excited by the scene.

On the set of 'Rope' (1948)
The ten-minute takes required a specially-built soft floor to keep the noise down, sets that flew apart as the camera moved and days of rehearsals for both cast and crew.

ABOVE
Publicity still for 'Under Capricorn' (1949)
In 19th century Australia Henrietta Flusky (Ingrid
Bergman) is romanced by her cousin Charles
Adare (Michael Wilding) much to the annoyance
of her ex-convict husband Sam (Joseph Cotten).

TOP LEFT
Still from 'Under Capricorn' (1949)
After years of depression and alcoholism,
Henrietta momentarily recaptures some of
her past glory at the Governor's ball.

LEFT
Still from 'Under Capricorn' (1949)
The housekeeper Milly (Margaret Leighton)
is secretly in love with Sam. She encourages
Henrietta to drink, places shrunken heads in
her bed and even tries to poison her.

OPPOSITE
Still from 'Under Capricorn' (1949)
Although the shrunken head is all too real
to Henrietta, everybody else thinks she is
demented.

Still from 'Stage Fright' (1950)
Jonny Cooper (Richard Todd) is on the run after
being framed for murder. Girlfriend Eve Gill
decides to investigate to clear his name.

On the set of 'Stage Fright' (1950)
Marlene Dietrich tries to attract her director's
attention.

In 1953, French critics told Hitchcock that he often used the transference of guilt from one character to another as the basis of his films. Thus, in his double chase movies the police transfer guilt to the innocent man on the run, who must transfer the guilt to one of the villains. This idea is at its most interesting when, as in *Blackmail*, *Sabotage*, *Strangers on a Train* and *I Confess*, the main character is to a certain extent guilty of a crime. In *Blackmail*, Alice is guilty of manslaughter but in the end the police transfer the guilt to Tracy, the blackmailer. Similarly, in *Sabotage* Winnie is guilty of killing her husband Karl but the police transfer it to the Professor when he blows up Karl's body. In *Strangers on a Train*, tennis ace Guy Haines humours Bruno Anthony when they meet on a train and in doing so seems to agree that it would be a good idea for them to swap killings and murder the person the other one hates. This initial misunderstanding is forgivable, but after Bruno kills Guy's estranged wife Guy does not go to the police because he is afraid of what the scandal will do to his political ambitions. Also, when Guy goes to kill Bruno's father at the prearranged time, his preparations imply that he is willing to carry out the murder, even if he reneges at the last moment. Guy is far from pure in his thoughts and actions and so his relationship with Bruno is more complicit than not.

Guilt is transferred to Father Logan, a Catholic priest, in *I Confess* (1953) when the murderer, Otto Keller, admits his crime under the sanctity of the holy sacrament of confession. This means that Father Logan is bound by his vows not to reveal the murderer even when he is accused of the crime. By coincidence, the victim, a lawyer named Vilette, was blackmailing Father Logan over an alleged affair he had with Ruth Grandfort, the wife of an important politician, before he took his vows.

The austere Father Logan, played with great dignity by Montgomery Clift, is silent for most of the film, echoing his refusal to talk to the police, yet Hitchcock and Clift still manage to convey Logan's inner thoughts. In one masterly scene, whilst a group of priests talk about some inane subject over breakfast, Hitchcock's camera concentrates on the faces of Logan and Alma Keller, whose looks develop the tension about whether or not Logan will reveal the killer. Montgomery Clift was from the method school of acting that stipulated that the actor must become the character to give a truthful portrayal. Often actors of this school would ask a director like Hitchcock what their motivation in a scene was and Hitchcock would give a glib reply like "to get to the other side of the room." For Hitchcock it was the camera that acted. When he famously said "actors should be treated like cattle" he meant that he treated actors as objects, like an artist paints fruit and flowers, and that he gives them meaning with his camera.

I Confess and *Strangers on a Train* were beautifully filmed thanks to the cinematography of Robert Burks, who went on to collaborate closely with Hitchcock on twelve films. Their next film was *Dial M for Murder* (1954), a straightforward adaptation of a stage play about Tony Wendice who wants to murder his wife Margot for money. As John Russell Taylor points out in his book *Hitch* (1978), *Dial M for Murder* has some similarities to *Strangers on a Train* that make it seem almost like a sequel to the former film: Tony Wendice is an ex-tennis professional who has married well, just as Guy Haines was a tennis player planning to marry the daughter of the politician that backed him; and like Bruno Anthony, Wendice blackmails Lesgate to do the killing for him and hence has an alibi.

'The thing that amuses me about Hitchcock is the way he directs a film in his head before he knows what the story is. You find yourself trying to rationalise the shots he wants to make rather than the story.'

Raymond Chandler[26]

OPPOSITE TOP LEFT
Still from 'Strangers on a Train' (1951)
Psychopath Bruno Anthony (Robert Walker) begins strangling a dinner guest for real when he sees Barbara Morton (Patricia Hitchcock, centre) who resembles the girl he killed, Miriam Haines.

OPPOSITE TOP RIGHT
Still from 'Strangers on a Train' (1951)
Guy Haines (Farley Granger) hangs on for dear life in the final merry-go round scene.

OPPOSITE BOTTOM LEFT
Still from 'Strangers on a Train' (1951)
When Guy Haines and Bruno Anthony meet on a train, Bruno suggests that they switch murders because nobody will suspect a complete stranger of being the murderer.

OPPOSITE BOTTOM RIGHT
On the set of 'Strangers on a Train' (1951)
Cinematographer Robert Burks and Alfred Hitchcock discuss a camera set-up under the merry-go-round.

ABOVE
On the set of 'I Confess' (1953)
Anne Baxter is doused in water in preparation for
the flashback scene. Montgomery Clift watches.

RIGHT
Still from 'I Confess' (1953)
Michael Logan (Montgomery Clift) and Ruth
Grandfort (Anne Baxter) have to find shelter
from the rain. The lawyer Vilette assumed they
made love.

ABOVE
On the set of 'I Confess' (1953)
Montgomery Clift and O. E. Hasse are in front of
the camera. Hitchcock got permission to film all
over Quebec City, including St Severin's Church
for this scene.

LEFT
Still from 'I Confess' (1953)
Otto Keller (O. E. Hasse) confessed a murder to
Father Michael Logan so Father Logan is bound
by his vows not to reveal this to anybody.

Overall, *Dial M for Murder* is a workmanlike and static film (most of it takes place in one room) occasionally enlivened by an extraordinary shot. For example, when Wendice is walking through the plan with Lesgate we see the apartment from directly above so that it becomes diagrammatical. The murder attempt on Margot is very dramatic and ends with Lesgate falling on the scissors in his back, forcing them into him in slow motion.

With the completion of *Dial M for Murder*, Hitchcock had finished a multi-picture deal with Warner Brothers. He then signed a phenomenal deal at Paramount Pictures, the terms of which meant that he would direct and produce five films, with ownership reverting to him after eight years. Both financially and creatively, Hitchcock now entered the most rewarding period of his life.

ABOVE
Still from 'Dial M for Murder' (1954)
Lesgate (Anthony Dawson) lies dead after attacking Margot Wendice (Grace Kelly). The attempted murder was arranged by Margot's husband.

OPPOSITE
On the set of 'I Confess' (1953)
By placing a glass of water on Brian Aherne, who plays Father Logan's attorney, Hitchcock creates a visual metaphor for the justice system.

'Perhaps [the common denominator of his films] lies in Hitchcock's fundamental distrust of the Law, not that the representatives of the Law are incapable of serving it, but that the letter of the Law itself is incapable of meeting the complex demands of justice and morality.'

David Rodowick [17]

129

Cameos

6

7

8

12

13

15

Long before his face and figure became known worldwide via his 1950s TV shows, Alfred Hitchcock was known through the cameo appearances he made in his films.

Hitch maintained that his first appearance, in *The Lodger* (1926), was borne out of practicality because he needed somebody to fill the foreground space in a newsroom and he was immediately available to fill it.

The cameo roles were a bit of fun at first and then became a superstition. Later, when the public expected to see Hitch he introduced the cameo as soon as possible so that they

could concentrate on the film rather than the cameo being a distraction.

The following numbered list of cameos correspond with the numbered images.

1/2. *The Lodger* (1926) This film has two Hitch appearances. First, he is seated at a news-room with his back to us. Later, wearing a cap, he is seen leaning against the railings when the lodger is trapped by the lynch mob.
3. *Blackmail* (1929) Trying to read a book on the underground train, Hitch (left) is bothered by a little boy. The boy was a little confused by the experience of filming this scene because he would be told to be naughty, then would be told off whilst filming, and then he would be given sweets when filming finished.
4. *Murder!* (1930) Hitch is a passer-by.
5. *The 39 Steps* (1935) Again Hitch is just a passer-by. This is a publicity image.

1

3

5

9

10

18

19

6. *Young and Innocent* (1937) Outside the courts, Hitch is a big press photographer with a tiny camera. This image shows the cameo about to be filmed.

7. *The Lady Vanishes* (1938) Hitch appears in a London railway station right at the end. He is difficult to spot.

8. *Rebecca* (1940) As Jack Favell (George Sanders) makes a call at a phone booth, Hitch walks by, but his face is hidden, so not much of a cameo. This image was taken for publicity purposes.

9. *Foreign Correspondent* (1940) Just before Jones (Joel McCrea) meets Van Meer, Hitch is seen reading a newspaper on the street.

10. *Saboteur* (1942) Hitch is at a news-stand but it's not obvious.

11. *Shadow of a Doubt* (1943) Hitch plays poker on the train and holds a full house. We don't see his face.

12. *Lifeboat* (1944) In one of the most ingenious cameos, as Gus (William Bendix) reads a newspaper, Hitch is seen in before and after photos for Reduco, a weight-reduction product.

13. *Spellbound* (1945) Hitch gets out of a crowded elevator smoking a cigar.

14. *Notorious* (1946) Hitch drinks champagne at the party. The irony is that in this film the MacGuffin is hidden in champagne bottles.

15. *The Paradine Case* (1947) Hitch leaves a train station carrying a cello case. He is behind Anthony Keane (Gregory Peck).

16. *Rope* (1948) Hitch's famous profile drawing is seen as a flashing neon sign advertising Reduco at the far right of the background. An enlargement from the set photo is shown.

17/18. *Under Capricorn* (1949) Hitch appears at the Governor's reception, and on the steps of Government House.

19. *Stage Fright* (1950) While Eve Gill (Jane Wyman) is walking along the street, practising her accent as Doris, Hitch walks past and looks back at her, wondering about her curious behaviour.

20. *Strangers on a Train* (1951) As Guy Haines (Farley Granger) is getting off a train, Hitch boards carrying a bass violin.

21. *I Confess* (1953) At the beginning, Hitch is seen crossing the street at the top of a long staircase.

22. *Dial M for Murder* (1954) Hitch is one of the people sitting at the right hand table in the class reunion photo.

23. *Rear Window* (1954) Hitch is seen winding a clock in the musician's apartment.

24. *To Catch a Thief* (1955) Hitch is on a bus, beside John Robie (Cary Grant), who looks at Hitch.

25. *The Trouble with Harry* (1955) Hitch walks past the outdoor art exhibition to the left of the picture. This is easy to miss unless you are looking at a widescreen print.

26. *The Man Who Knew Too Much* (1956) In the Marrakesh market, Hitch watches the acrobats, although again you need to see it in widescreen.

27. *The Wrong Man* (1956) Hitch introduces the film. He was originally to be seen in the diner with Sonny (Henry Fonda) but this was removed because Hitch thought it interfered with the documentary realism he was trying to invoke. The image is from the cut scene.

28. *Vertigo* (1958) Hitch walks by the entrance of the shipbuilding yard carrying a bugle case.

29. *North by Northwest* (1959) Just after the credits, Hitch runs to catch a bus but the door slams in his face.

23

24

28

29

35

36

30. *Psycho* (1960) Hitch stands outside Marlon Crane's office wearing a ten-gallon hat.
31. *The Birds* (1963) Near the beginning Hitch leaves the pet shop with two Scottie dogs.
32. *Marnie* (1964) Hitch is in the corridor of hotel where Marnie is staying.
33. *Torn Curtain* (1966) Hitch holds a baby in the lobby of a hotel in Copenhagen.
34. *Topaz* (1969) At the airport, Hitch is in a wheelchair, attended by a nurse (his long-time assistant Peggy Robertson) then he gets up to shake someone's hand.

35. *Frenzy* (1972) At the beginning, a crowd are listening to a political speech by the Thames when a dead body is spotted in the river. Hitch's cameo is as one of the onlookers trying to get a glimpse of the dead woman. This image was taken on the set.
36. *Family Plot* (1976) Hitch is seen in silhouette behind the door of the department of vital statistics. He seems to be gesturing rudely.

PAGES 134/135
"Have You Heard?" in 'Life' (13 July 1942)
Hitchcock was asked to direct a photo-drama to help the war effort, which he did with the aid of *Life* photographer Eliot Elisofon. *"Have You Heard?": The Story of Wartime Rumors* followed the movement of gossip from person to person resulting in the sinking of an American troopship. Hitchcock cameos as a bartender.

"An Absolute Master" 1954–1980

In the years from 1954 to 1960, Alfred Hitchcock produced and directed nine feature films and seventeen episodes for TV shows produced by his Shamley Productions. He introduced over 350 of the television shows that carried his name. As well as bringing him widespread fame and recognition, the TV shows allowed him to reap financial rewards by branding his name, image and reputation in other markets. His profile appeared on the cover of monthly short story digest *Alfred Hitchcock's Mystery Magazine*, which is still being published, and on over one hundred short story collections published over the next twenty years. Eighteen *Alfred Hitchcock and the Three Investigators* children's mysteries were also written, as well as short story records and a game called *Why?* In 1956 Hitchcock's personal income from his various endeavours was four million dollars and it was to rise over the coming years. He would later swap the rights to his TV shows for shares in Universal and became their third biggest stockholder. Yet, contrarily, Alma and Alfred lived in a comparatively modest home in Bel Air.

Hitchcock's prodigious output was more than matched by his creativity. It seemed that he could move from black comedy to documentary realism, from light-hearted action adventure to dark psychological thriller, without compromising his vision. However, it was during this period that the public's perception of Hitchcock as the 'Master of Suspense' became so entrenched that this was the only type of film that they would accept from him. Consequently, he became typecast and if he made films outside the confines of the genre he had made his own then he was mauled by critics and cinema-goers alike.

To a mainstream director working within the Hollywood system it must have come as quite a shock when he learnt that he was the darling of many French critics writing for *Cahiers du cinéma*. In the mid-1950s, they were putting forward the idea that the director, rather than the producer, writer or actors, was the author of the films he made, and this fitted with the perception that Hitchcock controlled every aspect of his films. Eric Rohmer and Claude Chabrol wrote a long study of Hitchcock, published in 1957, and François Truffaut carried out a booklength interview with Hitchcock, published in 1967. As well as proposing a different way of looking at and analysing film, these critics went on to form the

Alfred Hitchcock and François Truffaut (1962)
Truffaut, one of the leading lights of the 'auteur' theory and a director of the French New Wave, interviewed Hitchcock extensively for a seminal film book.

"A lot of people think I'm a monster – they really do, I've been told that!"
Alfred Hitchcock [28]

On the set of 'Rear Window' (1954)
On one level 'Rear Window' is a simple suspense picture, but on another it is about film-making. Jeff looks out of his window and makes up stories about the people he sees. These stories reflect Jeff's life and concerns, just as (we assume) Hitchcock's film reflect his life and concerns.

nucleus of the French New Wave, often invoking elements of Hitchcock's work in their films: Rohmer gave his view on obsession in *Le Genou de Claire* (*Claire's Knee*, 1970); Truffaut adapted American noir authors like David Goodis and Cornell Woolrich; and Chabrol made many thrillers in the Hitchcock mode like *Le Boucher* (*The Butcher*, 1970). These books established Hitchcock's reputation and were pathfinders for the vast number of books subsequently published about Hitchcock and his work.

Arguably, the complete creative control Hitchcock received at Paramount, combined with the ownership of the films reverting to Hitchcock after eight years, gave the director the greatest freedom he had ever experienced. As a result, he made the purest cinema of his career. Hitchcock told Truffaut: "In one of [Vsevolod Illareonovitch Pudovkin's] books on the art of montage, he describes an experiment by his teacher, [Lev] Kuleshov. You see a close-up of the Russian actor Ivan Mosjukhin. This is immediately followed by a shot of a dead baby. Back to Mosjukhin again and you read compassion on his face. Then you take

Publicity still for 'Rear Window' (1954)
While professional photographer Jeff (James
Stewart) spends his spare time looking into his
neighbours' windows, society girl Lisa (Grace
Kelly) tries to interest him in marriage.

away the dead baby and you show a plate of soup, and now, when you go back
to Mosjukhin, he looks hungry. Yet, in both cases, they use the same shot of the
actor; his face was exactly the same."[24] Hitchcock applied this technique in *Rear
Window* (1954) where Jeff, a photographer who is confined to a wheelchair with
a broken leg, whiles away the summer looking out his rear window to watch the
people in the adjoining apartments. Hitchcock has a shot of Jeff looking through
his camera, then a shot of the beautiful dancer, then Jeff. We perceive Jeff to be a
dirty old man. Hitch repeats the sequence, but replaces the dancer with a lonely
woman, and Jeff becomes a romantic.

Hitchcock's extraordinary achievement in *Rear Window* is that the whole
film is shot from Jeff's point of view from within his room (echoing his earlier
experiments with *Lifeboat* and *Rope*), yet it commands our complete involvement
because of our voyeuristic tendencies. Furthermore, when Jeff thinks that one of
the neighbours, Lars Thorwald, has killed his wife, cut her up and disposed of the
body, his fervour is such that we also wish this terrible thing to have happened.

"Mystery is mystifying; it is an intellectual thing.
Suspense is an emotional thing."

Alfred Hitchcock *

ABOVE
Publicity still for 'Rear Window' (1954)
The relationships lived behind each of the
windows reflect the possible futures waiting
for Jeff and Lisa's relationship.

RIGHT
On the set of 'Rear Window' (1954)
Alfred Hitchcock uses a radio to direct the
neighbours in their apartments while James
Stewart acts and Robert Burks films.

It is quite appropriate then that in the end Jeff pays for his evil thoughts (even though he is proved correct) by falling and breaking his other leg.

Although the thriller is at the forefront of the story, the film is really a love story between Jeff, who is reluctant to commit himself to a relationship, and his effervescent girlfriend Lisa. Each of the neighbours represents a permutation of the possible outcomes of the relationship between Jeff and Lisa. The dancer, nicknamed 'The Torso' by Jeff, is life and beauty personified, like Lisa. The newly-weds discover the joy of sex. The single woman, nicknamed 'Miss Lonelyhearts', needs love and suffers from a lack of it. The songwriter cannot sell his songs and is frustrated by his lack of success. The childless couple dote on their dog, which they treat like a child. The sculptress is so immersed in her work that she does not have time for a social life. Finally there is the travelling salesman Lars Thorwald and his invalid wife, a dark reflection of Lisa and the invalid Jeff, whose love goes awry with tragic consequences.

Lisa is the catalyst who persuades Jeff that she is the right girl for him. One scene begins with her suddenly approaching a dozing Jeff and kissing him awake in slow motion. As well as its erotic nature, the scene symbolises that Lisa takes the initiative and awakens Jeff to his love for her. When she goes to Lars' apartment looking for the wedding ring that will convict Lars of murder, Jeff is both afraid for her safety and attracted by her spirit. Lisa gets the ring and points to it on her finger to let Jeff know that he is right about the wife being murdered, but it can also be read as Lisa proposing marriage to Jeff. When Lisa is sent to jail, Jeff symbolically gives his camera for bail. The size and shape of the camera make it a phallic object, a symbol of male power, so when he emasculates himself by giving it up for her, he is showing her his true love.

If *Rear Window* can be seen as one woman's pursuit of a man, then *To Catch a Thief* (1955) went one better by having two women, Frances and Danielle, pursue John Robie, the former the jewel thief known as The Cat. Set in the French Riviera, Robie is accused of a series of jewel robberies that bear his unmistakable trademarks and is chased by the police. He investigates to clear his name, using American oil-millionairess Jessie Stevens and her daughter Frances as bait for the counterfeit Cat. The real attraction is the sexual chemistry between Robie and Frances, whose scenes together crackle with sexual innuendo.

Hitchcock designed the romances in his films so that the consummation of the relationship is as full of suspense as the action sequences. He explained to interviewers that he liked his films to feature an icy blonde in a business suit or dowdy clothing who appears uninterested in men, but who becomes a whore in the bedroom. To Hitchcock, "Sex should not be advertised." Invariably, at the beginning of the film the woman is distant and will not have anything to do with the man. She is filmed in a classical profile so that her eyes do not meet either the man or the audience. Her hair is tied up and perfectly coiffured. She exudes confidence and self-control. Then, when the man least expects it, she lowers her defences. In *To Catch a Thief*, Frances is cold towards Robie and when he accompanies her to the door of her room she unexpectedly puts her lips to his. Later, she is enticing him with her baubles, licking his fingers and they kiss to a crescendo of fireworks. Again, as in *Rear Window*, after Frances has proven herself to Robie by helping to capture the cat burglar, they plan to marry. The twist is that Frances' mother will be living with them!

ABOVE
Still from 'Rear Window' (1954)
When Lisa finds Mrs Thorwald's wedding ring (proving that Mrs Thorwald is dead), Lisa points to it to show Jeff. It is also a proposal of marriage.

PAGE 142
On the set of 'To Catch a Thief' (1955)
A stand-in helps to line up a rooftop shot. Note the ledge below him, out of shot, to break his fall if he slipped.

PAGE 143 TOP
On the set of 'To Catch a Thief' (1955)
Hitchcock looks on as Cary Grant and Grace Kelly kiss.

PAGE 143 BOTTOM
On the set of 'To Catch a Thief' (1955)
The tension is broken after the intense love scene.

ABOVE
Still from 'To Catch a Thief' (1955)
Frances Stevens (Grace Kelly) and ex-burglar
John Robie (Cary Grant) swap double entendres.
As a picnic Stevens offers Robie some cold
chicken: "Do you want a leg or a breast?"
Robie: "You make the choice."

RIGHT
Still from 'To Catch a Thief' (1955)
Danielle Foussard (Brigitte Auber), the daughter
of one of Robie's Resistance fighter friends, also
makes a play for Robie. Both women are trying to
'catch' the thief.

This type of woman was nothing new in Hitchcock films. In *The 39 Steps*, Pamela is introduced in a train carriage wearing a pair of glasses when she is roughly kissed by Hannay who wants to hide his face from the police. Dr Constance Peterson is a workaholic bespectacled psychiatrist in *Spellbound*. As the films progress, the ladylike manners or the shallowness (as in *The Lady Vanishes*) of the women are peeled away making them more human. The same is also true of men in Hitchcock's films, in that they stop acting like conceited children by the end of the film. As well as stripping his characters of their false faces, Hitchcock was also quite adept at removing the veneers of the actors and crew he worked with through practical jokes and withering comments. During production of *To Catch a Thief*, for example, Hitchcock was annoyed by the high-handed attitude of René Blanchard who played Commissioner Lepic and so one morning he wished Blanchard a good morning and asked if he slept well. "Yes, thank you," replied the actor. "And with whom, Monsieur?" asked Hitchcock. The French crew found this particularly funny and Hitchcock did not have to prick any more egos during the rest of the production.

The understatement of Hitchcock's women, and the way he gives the audience information that the characters do not possess to create suspense, results in the viewer experiencing a sense of intimacy. The spectator must put two and two together to work out what is happening and why. Hitchcock also liked understated humour, which led him to his next project, *The Trouble with Harry* (1955), an adaptation of a blackly comic novel by Jack Trevor Story. It was one of Hitchcock's favourite films because he found the nonchalant attitude of the characters to Harry's dead body amusing. One by one each of the characters find the body in the woods and assume that they killed him, and then attempt to conceal him. Over the course of a day Harry is buried and exhumed four times and two romances come to fruition.

The film is beautifully photographed to show the red and orange autumn foliage of Vermont to best effect. However, in reality most of those leaves were plastic and fixed to the trees after some terrible storms stripped the trees bare just prior to shooting. Also, even though Hitchcock liked to film on location, the adverse conditions meant that most of the sequences in the woods were recreated in the studio. Similarly on *The Man Who Knew Too Much* (1956), the remake of his 1934 film, although Hitchcock filmed on location in Marrakesh he still found it necessary to create specific shots back in Hollywood. For example, when Louis Bernard, wearing Arab robes, is knifed in the marketplace and whispers a secret message to Dr Ben McKenna, Hitch mixes a location shot in Marrakesh, a close-up of Bernard's face in Hollywood against a blank ground and sky, and a back projection of Marrakesh with actors in the foreground. This mix of real and unreal is common in Hitchcock's pictures and is part of his heightened visual style.

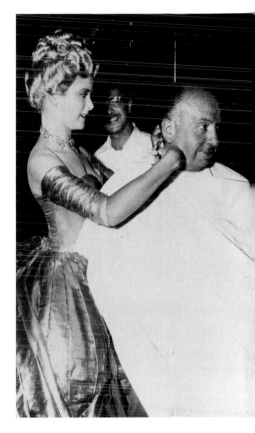

On the set of 'To Catch a Thief' (1955)
Grace Kelly attends to Hitchcock's follicles.

ABOVE
On the set of 'The Trouble with Harry' (1955)
Hitchcock with Shirley MacLaine and John Forsythe. The deadpan black comedy reflected Hitchcock's taste in humour. Unfortunately, it did not reflect the taste of most film-goers.

LEFT
Still from 'The Trouble with Harry' (1955)
Sam Marlowe (John Forsythe), Jennifer Rogers (Shirley MacLaine), Miss Gravely (Mildred Natwick) and Captain Albert Wiles (Edmund Gwenn) consider what to do with Harry Worp. The trouble is that Harry is dead and nobody knows who killed him.

OPPOSITE
Still from 'The Trouble with Harry' (1955)
Harry Worp (Philip Truex) is on ice whilst Arnie Rogers (Jerry Mathers) works out what to tell his mother.

PAGE 148
Still from 'The Man Who Knew Too Much' (1956)
Mr and Mrs Drayton (Bernard Miles and Brenda De Banzie) and Jo and Doctor Ben McKenna (Doris Day and James Stewart) witness the death of an Arab in Marrakesh. In fact, this is Louis Bernard , who passes on vital information to Ben before he dies.

PAGE 149
Still from 'The Man Who Knew Too Much' (1956)
Hank McKenna (Christopher Olsen) is threatened by a terrorist group. His life is forfeit if his parents help foil the assassination of a foreign Prime Minister.

Instead of the usual romantic element, Ben and Jo McKenna are bound together in *The Man Who Knew Too Much* by their love for their son Hank. Their initial bickering over Jo's former career as a singer hints at problems within the marriage. This is emphasised when Ben drugs Jo to knock her out as he tells her of Hank's kidnapping. This sinister act denies Jo the free will to react, and free will is the central theme of the film. The McKennas are given a simple choice. Either they stay silent about what Bernard told them, saving the life of their son but implicitly sentencing a foreign Prime Minister to death, or they tell the police what they know, saving the foreign Prime Minister but losing their son. The villains are effectively transferring any guilt to the parents. The most exciting and pivotal moment in the film is during the stunning ten-minute sequence at the Albert Hall. Whilst the music is playing, we watch Jo go through agony as she decides whether or not to save her child. She screams, putting off the assassin's aim and saving the foreign Prime Minister. There is a certain musical irony at the conclusion because Jo, who gave up her musical career to raise her son, sings a song at the Prime Minister's Embassy that Hank recognises and whistles back to her, leading him to safety.

Whilst Jo McKenna confronted her nightmare situation like a true heroine, in *The Wrong Man* (1956) Rose Balestrero falls apart and retreats into "a maze of terror" inside her head when her husband Manny is arrested and goes to trial for a series of robberies. The tragedy is that Manny is innocent and was arrested because he resembled the real robber.

Based on a true story, the film was shot in the actual locations and used the people involved to make the film as authentic as possible. Members of the Balestrero family were present on location and they helped rewrite the dialogue to accurately reflect what was said. However, there were still many distinctive Hitchcock touches. Much of the film is wordless because the camera follows Manny (Henry Fonda) wherever he goes, so we see the world from his perspective, including the polite, clean and respectable process of law, which is the villain of the piece. The police, the District Attorney, the courts and the jails all work together to break the family rather than protect it. This is ironic because at the beginning of the film Manny tells his family how lucky they are, and that they are the result of millions of years of evolution. Disillusioned by the world, Manny turns to his faith and prays for a miracle. As it happens, at that very moment the real robber is caught, implying that an act of God saved Manny from jail.

The Wrong Man was superbly photographed in a documentary style, and it is plain to see which elements of the case attracted Hitchcock so much. There is a mistaken identity, a man thrown into an evil environment, the helplessness of the central character and the idea of the doppelgänger or evil version of ourselves roaming the world. The doppelgänger was a strong recurring theme in Hitchcock's work and was evident in films like *Shadow of a Doubt*, *Strangers on a Train*, *Rear Window* and his next film, *Vertigo* (1958).

'[Hitchcock was] always meticulous in his attention to production details… [He] not only visited, measured and inspected every real-life locale of the story, but also had his staff record with stop-watch accuracy the way the subway ran at the time of the events depicted. … the block-by-block itinerary of the hero and the experience of all the principal characters in the drama.

Action that took place at night had to be re-enacted at night. Moreover, it had to be re-enacted in exactly the same way, in the very same spot.'

Frederic Foster [29]

ABOVE
Publicity still for 'The Wrong Man' (1956)
Everybody identifies Manny Balestrero (Henry Fonda) as an armed robber and his wife Rose (Vera Miles) cracks up from all the pressure.

LEFT
On the set of 'The Wrong Man' (1956)
Richard Robbins, who plays the real thief, chats with Henry Fonda. Notice the similar hats.

ABOVE
Still from 'Vertigo' (1958)
Gavin Elster (Tom Helmore) arranges for Scottie
to follow a double of his wife as part of a plot to
kill the real Madeleine.

LEFT
Still from 'Vertigo' (1958)
At the beginning of the film, police detective
Scottie Ferguson (James Stewart) suffers from
vertigo during a rooftop chase and a fellow
policeman dies trying to save him. Notice the
Golden Gate Bridge in the background.

At its heart, *Vertigo* is a gothic romance between Scottie and death. Scottie, an ex-police detective who is afraid of heights, is hired to follow Madeleine Elster wherever she goes, and he finds out that she believes herself to be the reincarnation of Carlotta Valdez, who was used by a man and then thrown out on the streets before committing suicide. After Madeleine tries to commit suicide at the Golden Gate Bridge, Scottie saves her and makes love to her. Madeleine then succeeds in committing suicide by jumping from the bell tower of a mission church. Scottie is unable to save her because his vertigo prevents him from climbing to the top of the bell tower. After a mental breakdown, Scottie returns to the world and sees Judy Barton, a woman who bears a remarkable resemblance to Madeleine. Scottie obsessively romances and remodels her, turning his new love into a reincarnation of Madeleine. When he discovers that Judy was in fact pretending to be Madeleine as part of an elaborate scheme to murder the real Madeleine, Scottie drags her to the top of the bell tower, defeating his vertigo. However, as they profess their love for each other, Judy cowers away from a shadow she thinks is the ghost of Madeleine and falls to her death, leaving Scottie wrought with guilt and woe, repeating the cycle of love and death intertwined.

The key to this extraordinary film is when Scottie and Madeleine visit the sequoias. A cross-section of an old tree trunk is marked with labels showing history repeating itself through wars and treaties. It is then that we learn that sequoia translates as 'always green, everlasting', which Hitchcock uses as a Rosetta Stone. When we first see Madeleine and then later first see her as Judy Barton, she is wearing green and in profile. Madeleine drives a green car and green from a neon light bathes Judy when she is transformed back into Madeleine. Carlotta, Madeleine and Judy are objects of love, remade, over and over. Such is the power of the film and Scottie's obsessive love that we quite forget that Gavin Elster goes unpunished for the murder of his wife.

Hitchcock relied heavily on unspoken information in his films. He also needed a substantial level of trust from his audience, and required them to extract the correct information from the films and build their own stories. Long sections of *Rear Window*, *Vertigo* and *Psycho* are wordless, yet there is no loss of understanding or involvement. In addition, Hitchcock often uses silence or only distant ambient noise for his soundscapes during dramatic moments like the strangling of Guy's wife in *Strangers on a Train* or Fry hanging by a thread from the Statue of Liberty in *Saboteur*. Perhaps his greatest use of silence was the aeroplane attack on Roger Thornhill in *North by Northwest*. Hitchcock came up with the idea, as he often did, as a way of avoiding clichés. Instead of being attacked in a dark, enclosed space, Thornhill was attacked in a bright, open space. This simple scene only works because of complex suspense elements in the rhythm of events and cutting. The lone man running from an unseen enemy who is attacking him for no apparent reason is a central motif in Hitchcock's work.

ABOVE
Still from 'Vertigo' (1958)
Having lost Madeleine to suicide, 'Scottie' Ferguson (James Stewart) tries to turn Judy Barton (Kim Novak) into the image of his lost love. Hitchcock places his characters in front of mirrors to echo the theme of the film.

OPPOSITE
Still from 'Vertigo' (1958)
Scottie's fear of heights (symbolically, his fear of committing to relationships) lost him Madeleine. He conquers this fear with Judy.

"The large mirrors do in fact serve the motif of doubled and split image. The mirrors are strategically placed in the flower shop, the department store, Ernie's Restaurant and more prominently in Novak's hotel room where she is transformed for the second time in the film into a man's idealised double, a fantasised image."

Henry Bumstead, Art Director

"I think that montage is the essential thing in a motion picture."

Alfred Hitchcock [4]

On the set of 'Vertigo' (1958)
Like Scottie, Hitchcock also moulded his female actresses into his very specific ideal of the icy blonde. Here Kim Novak takes direction from an animated Hitchcock.

North by Northwest begins as a case of mistaken identity when Thornhill is assumed to be George Kaplan. It later transpires that Kaplan does not exist and is a dummy agent created to divert Vandamm and the villains away from the FBI agent who has infiltrated them. In the grand tradition of *The 39 Steps*, *Young and Innocent* and *Sabotage*, Thornhill must clear his name by adopting different identities. There is even a MacGuffin in the form of microfilm in a statue, which is overshadowed by Thornhill's pursuit of the beautiful Eve Kendall, who is Vandamm's love interest and also happens to be an FBI agent. Eve plays hard to get by sending Thornhill to his death by crop duster aeroplane and then later shoots him in front of Vandamm. It is the biggest, fastest and most beautiful of Hitchcock's chase movies and it reaped dividends at the box office.

Hitchcock always kept an eye on the film industry and noticed that many shocking horror films, the type often played at drive-ins and derided by film critics, made a lot of profit because they were so cheap to make. He wondered what it would be like to make such a movie and even put up the money to produce one independently. Yet again, Hitchcock was experimenting. The film became *Psycho* (1960), a black comedy about a psychopath, with no shortage of sex and violence.

In *Psycho*, Hitchcock includes many of the motifs and techniques he had developed over a lifetime of film-making, but he utilises them to different effect. Marion Crane steals $40,000 from her employer and runs away to her lover but has to stay over at the Bates motel. Feeling increasingly guilty about her actions, Marion's talk with the shy Norman Bates leads to her decision to return the money. "I think we're all in our own private traps," Norman says, "We all go a little mad sometimes." Then she is killed in the shower, seemingly by Norman Bates' mother.

As with *Vertigo*, the death of the central female character occurs half-way through the film and then the real story of the film is revealed. We see Norman meticulously clean up the shower and dispose of the body like the good son he is. Such is the shock of the killing that for the rest of the film the audience has a heightened sense of fear and dread. Hitchcock designed the film, again rather like *Vertigo*, so that the suspense is maintained to the very end. The film was a box-office smash and instigated thousands of cinematic murders in the following decades.

There is no emotional attachment to any single character after Marion's death because Hitchcock does not develop the other characters or dwell on them long enough. In *The Birds* (1963) however, the film that followed *Psycho*, Hitchcock worried about that aspect during filming and so he began to improvise and rewrite on the set. This was something he had not done to such an extent for a long time but he found the process exciting and the result more rewarding. The characters are attacked by birds for no apparent reason and it irrevocably changes them. The domineering Mrs Brenner, who resents Melanie Daniels' attentions towards her son Mitch, is turned into a nervous wreck by the attacks. Meanwhile Melanie, who is introduced as a shallow selfish woman, comforts Mrs Brenner and then undergoes an ordeal trapped in a room of attacking birds. Like Lisa in *Rear Window*, the act of bravery wins her the man she loves. Once again, Hitchcock crystallised the romantic story to give strength to the dramatic one. The ending is reflective and unresolved, with the characters driving off into the dis-

Q: *Near the beginning [of* North by Northwest*], in the mad car race, one knows that Cary Grant can't be killed this early. So why is one excited?*

Hitchcock: *That again is purely the use of film in terms of the substitution of the language of the camera for words... It's the mode of expression. And the use of the size of the image. And the juxtaposition of different pieces of film to create emotion in a person. And you can make it strong enough to make them forget reason. You see, when you say that Cary Grant can't possibly be killed so early in the film, that's the application of reason. But you're not permitted to reason. Because the film should be stronger than reason.*[6]

OPPOSITE TOP
Still from 'North by Northwest' (1959)
Roger Thornhill (Cary Grant) runs for his life in one of Hitchcock's most memorable sequences.

OPPOSITE BOTTOM
Still from 'North by Northwest' (1959)
The crop-duster sequence ends with a bang.

159

ABOVE
Still from 'North by Northwest' (1959)
Roger Thornhill and Eve Kendall (Eva Marie Saint) in a deadly embrace. We are never sure which side Eve is working for.

LEFT
Still from 'North by Northwest' (1959)
Leonard (Martin Landau, right) watches Eve, who is in the arms of Vandamm (James Mason). Eve watches the MacGuffin, i. e. the statue containing the microfilm.

OPPOSITE
On the set of 'North by Northwest' (1959)
Cary Grant and Alfred Hitchcock discuss the murder of Townsend in the lobby of the United Nations building. The set was built using photos obtained by assistants visiting the building posing as tourists.

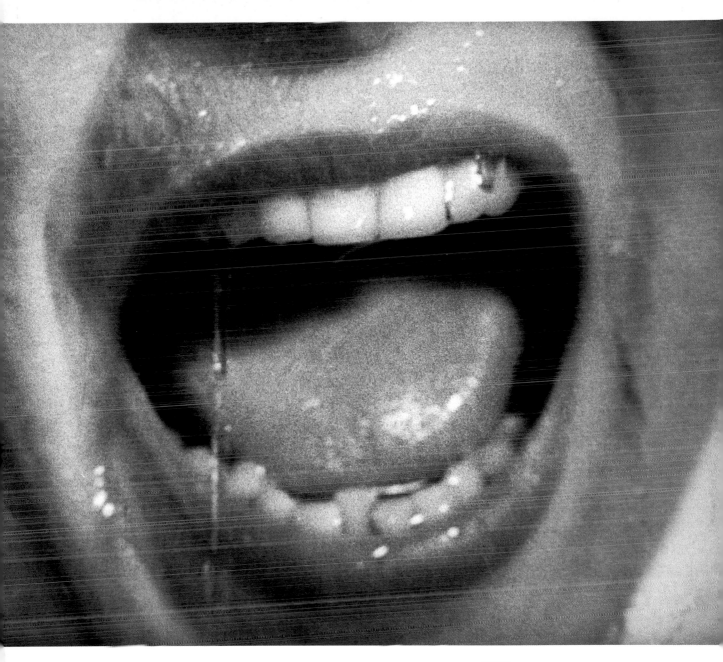

ABOVE
Still from 'Psycho' (1960)
The primal scream of Marion Crane (Janet Leigh).

OPPOSITE
On the set of 'Psycho' (1960)
Alfred Hitchcock directs a frightened Janet Leigh in the shower scene. The seventy-eight shots that edit into forty-five seconds of screen time took seven working days to complete.

Still from 'Psycho' (1960)
Mrs Bates.

Still from 'Psycho' (1960)
Norman Bates (Anthony Perkins) is a shy,
awkward boy who respects his mother and
wouldn't hurt a fly.

tance surrounded by thousands of birds. The people are trapped by forces beyond their control and there is nothing they can do about it.

In general, Hitch's movies were a series of set pieces linked together by plot. They were not character-driven. This meant that they relied on major stars to carry the emotion of the story. From the early 1960s, Hitch was without Cary Grant and James Stewart, and most of the famous actors who were from the emerging method school wanted the character's development to be the central focus. In addition, Hitch was losing control of his performers. He would develop a project around a big star, like Cary Grant or Audrey Hepburn, and then the star would drop out for one reason or another. Hitch tried to combat this by creating a star of his own in the form of Tippi Hedren, who played Melanie Daniels in *The Birds*. However, he exerted so much control over her during the making of *Marnie* (1964) that she rebelled against him and they never talked to each other again.

In a story more than a little reminiscent of *Spellbound*, when Marnie sees red she is compelled to steal money, after which she changes her identity. When she is caught by employer Mark Rutland, he forces her to marry him and rapes her on their honeymoon after he finds out she is frigid. He is as disturbed as she is, although this is never highlighted or developed sufficiently. Eventually they find out that Marnie was emotionally scarred when she killed a sailor as a child. There is a real sense that Hitchcock is out of his time with this film, and the casting of Sean Connery as Mark Rutland does not work primarily because Connery is best when playing loners.

There is a similar problem with Paul Newman in *Torn Curtain* (1966), who is wholly unconvincing playing physicist Professor Michael Armstrong opposite Julie Andrews as his fiancée, Sarah Sherman. When Armstrong defects to East Germany, it is a ruse to get a formula out of Professor Lindt's head. Once Michael has it, he and Sarah must escape back to the West. It is a good premise but Hitchcock makes the mistake of resolving the romantic tension between the lovers halfway through the film rather than developing it in tandem with the final chase.

However, as in any Hitchcock film, there is always a moment that stands out. In *Torn Curtain* it is when Michael and the farmer's wife murder Michael's bodyguard Gromek in the farmhouse. It is not as easy to kill someone as one might think. If they use a gun, the taxi driver outside would hear the noise. The attempt to use a knife fails as Michael and Gromek rotate and sway too quickly for the woman to be accurate, and once the knife is in Gromek, it snaps off. Next a spade is applied to Gromek's legs. When he falls to the floor, the woman opens the oven and turns on the gas. They slowly drag Gromek to it, put his head in and, in a high shot looking down, we see Gromek's hands flail about, twitch and stop. The farmer's wife picks up the spade to indicate that she will bury both Gromek and his motorbike.

The loss of quality in Hitchcock's films around this period can be traced to the rapid erosion of the close-knit team that he had built up during the 1950s. Hitchcock had such trust in cinematographer Robert Burks that he did not even look into the camera during filming. Apart from *Psycho*, Burks had worked on every Hitchcock film since *Strangers on a Train*, but he tragically died in a domestic fire after completing *Marnie*. It was a personal as well as professional loss to

The Birds: *'The ambiguity of the film's meaning is a prime virtue. If it had a specific allegorical meaning, it would have a particular relevance to each spectator who could then deal with it on its own level. But its very ambiguity makes the threat operate at every level of audience consciousness.'*

Ian Cameron & Richard Jeffrey [70]

Publicity still for 'The Birds' (1963)
Melanie Daniels (Tippi Hedren) is attacked by birds and is severely traumatised by the ordeal

Q: What would you say was the theme of
[The Birds]?

Hitchcock: If you like you can make it the theme
of too much complacency in the world: that
people are unaware that catastrophe surrounds
us all.[6]

On the set of 'The Birds' (1963)
Hitchcock has fun with the cast and crew. Note
the 'bird wrangler' on the right, who looks slightly
outnumbered.

On the set of 'Marnie' (1964)
Hitchcock clowns with cinematographer Robert Burks. They worked together from 'Strangers on a Train' until 'Marnie'.

Hitchcock. *Marnie* was also the last Hitchcock film for editor George Tomasini and composer Bernard Herrmann.

Although saddened by the financial failures of *Marnie* and *Torn Curtain*, Hitchcock knew that he had to find a new approach to film, as he had with *Psycho*. He commissioned a screenplay, still photos and almost an hour of location filming for *Kaleidoscope*, a film about a handsome young murderer who is hunted down by a woman. Featuring hippies in New York and influenced by the fluid camerawork of Michelangelo Antonioni's films, this would undoubtedly have put Hitchcock in the forefront of cutting-edge cinema, but Universal studios stopped it and made him direct *Topaz* (1969), perhaps the low point of his career. Based on a best-selling novel by Leon Uris, *Topaz* is the story of Soviet spies operating within General De Gaulle's French Intelligence. Besieged by technical problems, multiple storylines and a huge cast, the film that resulted was bland and tedious.

LEFT
Still from 'Marnie' (1964)
Mark Rutland (Sean Connery) is a predatory male who is attracted to and wants to possess the psychologically disturbed thief Marnie Edgar (Tippi Hedren). His desire for power is such that he rapes her on their honeymoon.

BELOW
On the set of 'Marnie' (1964)
The relationship between Hitchcock and Hedren was unbearably tense. After a row they did not talk to each other directly for the rest of the filming.

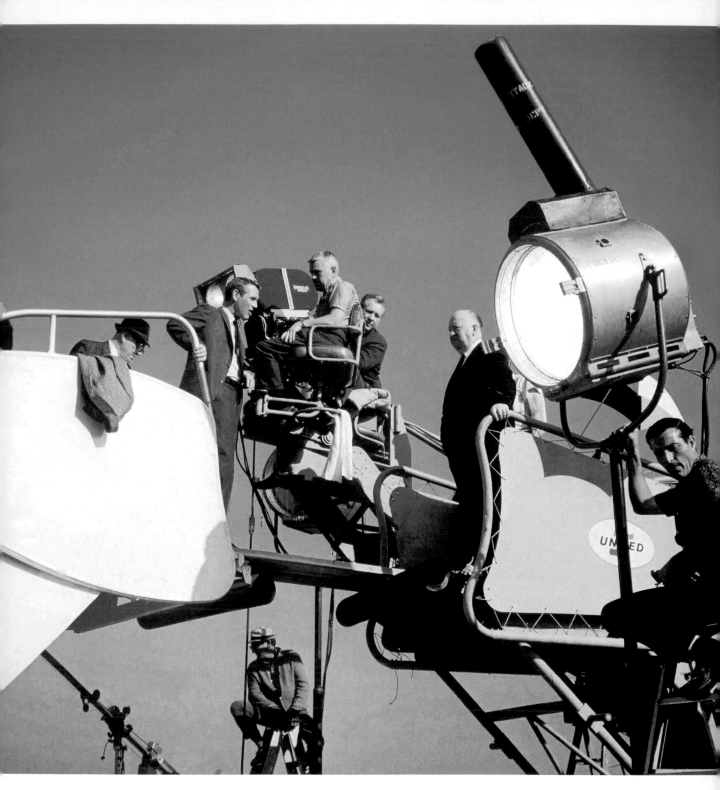

On the set of 'Torn Curtain' (1966)
Paul Newman and Hitchcock continue working
on a production neither was enthusiastic about.
They both knew that the script did not live up to
the exciting storyline.

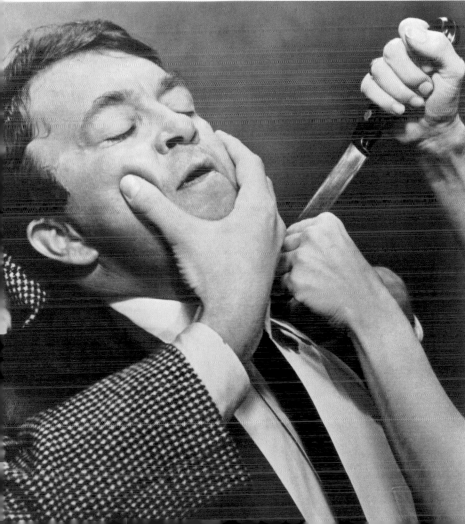

ABOVE
On the set of 'Torn Curtain' (1966)
Paul Newman watches as Hitchcock frames Julie Andrews. This told both the cast and crew what is to be seen on the screen.

LEFT
Still from 'Torn Curtain' (1966)
Hitchcock wanted to show how difficult it was to kill somebody. Here Hermann Gromek (Wolfgang Kieling) is being held by Professor Michael Armstrong and stabbed by a farmer's wife.

"I got the idea [for Torn Curtain*] from the disappearance of the two British diplomats, Burgess and MacLean, who deserted their country and went to Russia. I said to myself, 'What did Mrs MacLean think of the whole thing?' So you see, the first third of the film is more or less from a woman's point of view, until we have the dramatic showdown between the young couple in the hotel room in Berlin. From here on I take Paul Newman's point of view."*

Alfred Hitchcock [24]

ABOVE
Still from 'Topaz' (1969)
The final duel of honour was filmed but preview audiences laughed at it so it was hastily replaced.

OPPOSITE
Still from 'Topaz' (1969)
Hitchcock continued to infuse his work with resonant images In this case, the dead spies evoke the pietà, as had an image in 'The Lodger'. However, 'Topaz' lacked the emotional dynamics of his best films, and so these scattered images are the only evidence that a master was at work.

"It's only a movie."

Alfred Hitchcock[4]

On the set of 'Frenzy' (1972)
Filming the opening shot where a helicopter flies up the River Thames and zooms in on a political rally.

Frenzy (1972) was much more to Hitchcock's taste. Being the son of a London greengrocer, it is perhaps not surprising that Hitchcock had visualised a story showing twenty-four hours in a city from the perspective of food. First you would see the arrival of the food, then its preparation, the cooking of it, the eating of it and finally it being disposed of, leaving the city via the sewerage network. This, Hitchcock assured Truffaut, would visualise his theme of the rottenness of humanity. He never got to make the film but he did get to explore the world of the greengrocer in *Frenzy*, the story of a charming psychopathic killer and the surly, snarling unsympathetic man he frames for the murders. The killer, Bob Rusk, is a grocer in Covent Garden and on one occasion he has to get into a truck full of potato bags to retrieve a tiepin he had left on one of the victims. Meanwhile the diligent Inspector Oxford has to endure the horrible nightly meal prepared by his wife. This is a true return to form, with a harrowing sequence of rape and murder, and lots of suspense when the innocent Richard Blaney is sent to jail for murder.

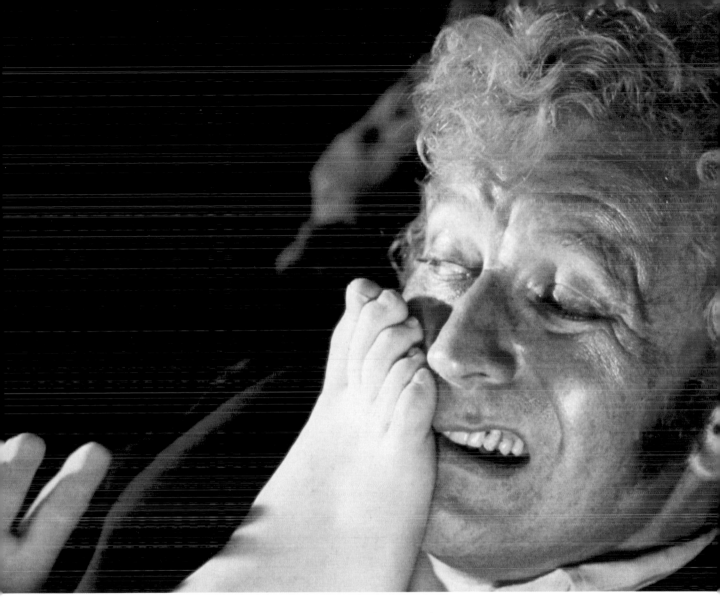

Finally, Hitchcock directed *Family Plot* (1976), a likeable thriller about a lost son who is due to inherit a fortune. Unfortunately, the couple tracking him down do not know that the lost son is a criminal mastermind and much criminal fun ensues. The film ends with a knowing wink to camera, a fitting end to a career that was laced with humour as well as murder and romance. After working for some time on *The Short Night*, a script based on the British spy George Blake who escaped from prison and was helped out of the country by gangland London, Hitch eventually gave in to his failing health and made the decision to stop making films in May 1979. He was given a knighthood in the Queen's New Year's Honours List and was feted by the American Film Institute but he had lost the will to film and directed his final fade-out on 29 April 1980.

Still from 'Frenzy' (1972)
Psychopath Bob Rusk (Barry Foster) inadvertently leaves his tiepin on a victim dumped in a potato truck. He retrieves it in a tense scene where Hitchcock made the audience complicit with the killer.

ABOVE
On the set of 'Family Plot' (1976)
Hitchcock watches Bruce Dern at work. Hitch-
cock planned complicated camera movements
through the graveyard. Dern said that, "For
Hitchcock, movement is dramatic. Not acting.
When he wants the audience emotionally moved,
the camera moves."

RIGHT
Still from 'Family Plot' (1976)
The plot revolves around finding Edward
Shoebridge, who has a large inheritance due
to him.

ABOVE
Still from 'Family Plot' (1976)
George Lumley (Bruce Dern) and Blanche Tyler (Barbara Harris) are on the trail of Edward Shoebridge, but it looks like somebody does not want him found.

LEFT
Still from 'Family Plot' (1976)
Arthur Adamson (William Devane) and Fran (Karen Black) are kidnappers whose lives eventually become intertwined with those of George and Blanche.

PAGES 180/181
On the set of 'Family Plot' (1976)
Hitchcock amuses Bruce Dern (right) between takes. Dern once commented that Hitchcock was a subtle man and the best actor he ever worked with.

Filmography

The Pleasure Garden *(1925)*
Crew: *Director* Alfred Hitchcock, *Screenplay* Eliot Stannard, *Novel* Oliver Sandys, *Producers* Michael Balcon & Erich Pommer, *Cinematographer* Baron Ventimiglia, *Assistant Director* Alma Reville, B&W, Silent, c. 85 mins.
Cast: Virginia Valli (Patsy Brand), Carmelita Geraghty (Jill Cheyne), Miles Mander (Levett), John Stuart (Hugh Fielding)

The Mountain Eagle *(1926)*
Crew: *Director* Alfred Hitchcock, *Screenplay* Eliot Stannard, *Producer* Michael Balcon, *Cinematographer* Baron Ventimiglia, B&W, Silent, c. 89 mins.
Cast: Nita Naldi (Beatrice), Bernhard Goetzke (Pettigrew), John F. Hamilton (Edward Pettigrew), Malcolm Keen (Fear o' God Fulton)

The Lodger *(1926)*
Crew: *Director* Alfred Hitchcock, *Screenplay* Eliot Stannard & Alfred Hitchcock, *Novel* Marie Belloc Lowndes, *Producers* Michael Balcon & Carlyle Blackwell Sr., *Cinematographer* Baron Ventimiglia, *Film Editing* Ivor Montagu, *Assistant Director* Alma Reville, *Editing/Titling* Ivor Montagu, *Title Designer* E. McKnight Kauffer, B&W, Silent, c. 100 mins.
Cast: Ivor Novello (The Lodger), June Tripp (Daisy Bunting, a Mannequin), Malcolm Keen (Joe Betts, a Police Detective), Marie Ault (The Landlady, Mrs Bunting), Arthur Chesney (Her Husband, Mr Bunting), Helena Pick (Anne Rowley)

Downhill *(1927)*
Crew: *Director* Alfred Hitchcock, *Screenplay* Eliot Stannard, *Play* David Lestrange (pseudonym for Constance Collier & Ivor Novello), *Producer* Michael Balcon, *Cinematographer* Claude L. McDonnell, *Film Editing* Ivor Montagu, B&W, Silent, c. 105 mins.
Cast: Ivor Novello (Roddy Berwick), Robin Irvine (Tim Wakely), Lilian Braithwaite (Lady Berwick), Isabel Jeans (Julia Hannah Jones), Ian Hunter (Archie), Sybil Rhoda (Sybil Wakely), Ben Webster (Doctor Dowson)
US Title: *When Boys Leave Home*

Easy Virtue *(1927)*
Crew: *Director* Alfred Hitchcock, *Screenplay* Eliot Stannard, *Play* Noel Coward, *Producer* Michael Balcon, *Cinematographer* Claude L. McDonnell, *Film Editing* Ivor Montagu, B&W, Silent, c. 105 mins.
Cast: Isabel Jeans (Larita Filton), Franklin Dyall (Her husband, M. Filton), Ian Hunter (The Plaintiff's Counsel), Robin Irvine (John Whittaker), Violet Farebrother (His mother), Eric Bransby Williams (The Corespondent)

The Ring *(1927)*
Crew: *Director & Scenario* Alfred Hitchcock, *Adaptation* Alma Reville, *Producer* John Maxwell, *Cinematographer* Jack E. Cox, B&W, Silent, c. 110 mins.
Cast: Carl Brisson (Jack Sanders aka One Round Jack), Lillian Hall-Davis (Mabel), Ian Hunter (Bob Corby, The Champion)

The Manxman *(1928)*
Crew: *Director* Alfred Hitchcock, *Screenplay* Eliot Stannard, *Novel* Hall Caine, *Producer* John Maxwell, *Cinematographer* Jack E. Cox, *Film Editing* Emile de Ruelle, *Still Photographer* Michael Powell, B&W, Silent, c. 100 mins.
Cast: Anny Ondra (Kate Cregeen), Carl Brisson (Pete Quilliam), Malcolm Keen (Philip Christian), Randle Ayrton (Caesar Cregeen), Clare Greet (Mother)

The Farmer's Wife *(1928)*
Crew: *Director* Alfred Hitchcock, *Screenplay* Leslie Arliss & Alfred Hitchcock & J.E. Hunter & Norman Lee & Eliot Stannard, *Play* Eden Philpotts, *Producer* John Maxwell, *Cinematographer* Jack E. Cox, *Film Editing* Alfred Booth, B&W, Silent, c. 100 mins.
Cast: Jameson Thomas (Farmer Samuel Sweetland), Lillian Hall-Davis (Araminta Dench, the Housekeeper)

Champagne *(1928)*
Crew: *Director* Alfred Hitchcock, *Screenplay* Eliot Stannard, *Story* Walter C. Mycroft, *Adaptation* Alfred Hitchcock, *Producer* John Maxwell, *Cinematographer* Jack E. Cox, *Still Photographer* Michael Powell, B&W, Silent, c. 104 mins.
Cast: Betty Balfour (Betty), Jean Bradin (The Boy), Theo von Alten (The Man), Gordon Harker (The Father)

Blackmail *(1929)*
Crew: *Director & Screenplay* Alfred Hitchcock, *Dialogue* Benn W. Levy & Michael Powell, *Play* Charles Bennett, *Producer* John Maxwell, *Original Music* Hubert Bath & Campbell Connelly, *Cinematographer* Jack E. Cox, *Film Editing* Emile de Ruelle, B&W, c. 80 mins.
Cast: Anny Ondra (Alice White), Joan Barry (Voice of Alice White), Sara Allgood (Mrs White), Charles Paton (Mr White), John Longden (Detective Frank Webber), Donald Calthrop (Tracy, the Blackmailer), Cyril Ritchard (The Artist)

Elstree Calling *(1930)*
Crew: *Directors* André Charlot & Alfred Hitchcock (some sketches) & Jack Hulbert & Paul Murray, *Screenplay* Val Valentine, *Original Music* Reg Casson & Vivian Ellis & Chic Endor, *Lyrics* Ivor Novello & Jack Strachey Parsons, *Cinematographer* Claude Friese-Greene, *Supervising Director* Adrian Brunel, B&W, 86 mins.
Cast: Donald Calthrop, Gordon Harker, Nathan Shacknovsky, John Stuart, Jameson Thomas, Anna May Wong (Herself)

Juno and the Paycock *(1930)*
Crew: *Director* Alfred Hitchcock, *Screenplay* Alfred Hitchcock & Alma Reville, *Play* Sean O'Casey, *Producer* John Maxwell, *Cinematographer* Jack E. Cox, *Film Editing* Emile de Ruelle, B&W, 85 mins.
Cast: Sara Allgood (Juno), Edward Chapman (Captain Boyle), Maire O'Neill (Mrs Madigan), Sidney Morgan (Joxer), John Longden (Chris Bentham), John Laurie (Johnny Boyle), Donald Calthrop (Needle Nugent), Barry Fitzgerald (The Orator)

Murder! *(1930)*
Crew: *Director* Alfred Hitchcock, *Adaptation* Alfred Hitchcock & Walter C. Mycroft, *Screenplay* Alma Reville, *Novel Enter Sir John* Clemence Dane & Helen Simpson, *Producer* John Maxwell, *Original Music* John Reynders, *Cinematographer* Jack E. Cox, *Film Editing* Rene Marrison & Emile de Ruelle, B&W, 100 mins.

Cast: Herbert Marshall (Sir John Menier), Norah Baring (Diana Baring), Phyllis Konstam (Doucie Markham, Doucebelle Dear), Edward Chapman (Ted Markham), Miles Mander (Gordon Druce), Esmé Percy (Handel Fane), Donald Calthrop (Ion Stewart), Clare Greet (Jury Member)

Mary (1930)

German version of *Murder!* directed by Hitchcock.

The Skin Game (1931)

Crew: *Director & Adaptation* Alfred Hitchcock, *Screenplay* Alma Reville, *Play* John Galsworthy, *Producer* John Maxwell, *Cinematographer* Jack E. Cox, *Film Editing* A. Gobett, *Clapper Boy* Jack Cardiff, B&W, 89 mins.
Cast: C. V. France (Mr Hillcrest), Helen Haye (Mrs Hillcrest), Jill Esmond (Jill Hillcrest), Edmund Gwenn (Mr Hornblower), John Longden (Charles Hornblower), Phyllis Konstam (Chloe Hornblower), Frank Lawton (Rolf Hornblower), Herbert Ross (Mr Jackman), Dora Gregory (Mrs Jackman), Edward Chapman (Dawker)

Rich and Strange (1932)

Crew: *Director & Adaptation* Alfred Hitchcock, *Screenplay* Alma Reville, *Additional Dialogue* Val Valentine, *Idea* Dale Collins, *Producer* John Maxwell, *Original Music* Hal Dolphe, *Musical Director* John Reynders, *Cinematographers* Jack E. Cox & Charles Martin, *Film Editing* Winifred Cooper & Rene Marrison, B&W, 87 mins.
Cast: Henry Kendall (Fred Hill), Joan Barry (Emily Hill), Percy Marmont (Commander Gordon), Betty Amann (The Princess), Elsie Randolph (The Old Maid), Aubrey Dexter (Colonel)
US Title: *East of Shanghai*

Number Seventeen (1932)

Crew: *Director* Alfred Hitchcock, *Screenplay* Rodney Ackland & Alfred Hitchcock & Alma Reville, *Novel* Joseph Jefferson Farjeon, *Producer* John Maxwell, *Original Music* A. Hallis, *Cinematographers* Jack E. Cox & Bryan Langley, *Film Editing* A. C. Hammond, B&W, 65 mins.
Cast: Leon M. Lion (Ben), Anne Grey (The Girl), John Stuart (The Detective), Donald Calthrop (Brant), Barry Jones (Henry Doyle), Ann Casson (Rose Ackroyd), Henry Caine (Mr Ackroyd), Garry Marsh (Sheldrake)

Waltzes from Vienna (1933)

Crew: *Director* Alfred Hitchcock, *Screenplay* Guy Bolton & Alma Reville, *Play* Guy Bolton, *Music* Johann Strauss Sr. & Johann Strauss, *Cinematographer* Glen MacWilliams, B&W, 80 mins.
Cast: Hindle Edgar (Leopold), Sybil Grove (Mme Fouchett), Edmund Gwenn (Strauss the Elder), Robert Hale (Ebezeder), Esmond Knight (Strauss the Younger), Jessie Matthews (Rasi), Frank Vosper (The Prince)
US Title: *Strauss' Great Waltz*

The Man Who Knew Too Much (1934)

Crew: *Director* Alfred Hitchcock, *Scenario* Edwin Greenwood & A.R. Rawlinson, *Additional Dialogue* Charles Bennett & D.B. Wyndham-Lewis &

Emlyn Williams, *Producers* Michael Balcon & Ivor Montagu, *Original Music* Arthur Benjamin, *Musical Director* Louis Levy, *Cinematographer* Curt Courant, *Film Editing* Hugh Stewart, B&W, 85 mins.
Cast: Leslie Banks (Bob Lawrence), Edna Best (Jill Lawrence), Peter Lorre (Abbott), Frank Vosper (Ramon), Hugh Wakefield (Clive), Nova Pilbeam (Betty Lawrence), Pierre Fresnay (Louis Bernard), Joan Harrison (Secretary)

The 39 Steps (1935)

Crew: *Director* Alfred Hitchcock, *Adaptation* Charles Bennett, *Continuity* Alma Reville, *Dialogue* Ian Hay, *Novel* John Buchan, *Producers* Michael Balcon & Ivor Montagu, *Original Music* Hubert Bath, *Musical Director* Louis Levy, *Cinematographer* Bernard Knowles, *Film Editing* Derek N. Twist, B&W, 81 mins.
Cast: Robert Donat (Richard Hannay), Madeleine Carroll (Pamela), Lucie Mannheim (Annabella Smith), Godfrey Tearle (Professor Jordan), Peggy Ashcroft (Margaret), John Laurie (John), Helen Haye (Mrs Jordan), Wylie Watson (Mr Memory), Gus McNaughton (Commercial Traveller)

Secret Agent (1936)

Crew: *Director* Alfred Hitchcock, *Scenario* Charles Bennett, *Dialogue* Ian Hay, *Additional*

Dialogue Jesse Lasky Jr. & Alma Reville, *Play* Campbell Dixon, *Novel Ashenden* W. Somerset Maugham, *Producers* Michael Balcon & Ivor Montagu, *Cinematographer* Bernard Knowles, *Film Editing* Charles Frend, B&W, 83 mins.
Cast: John Gielgud (Edgar Brodie/Richard Ashenden), Peter Lorre (The General), Madeleine Carroll (Elsa Carrington), Robert Young (Robert Marvin),

Percy Marmont (Caypor), Florence Kahn (Mrs Caypor), Charles Carson ('R'), Lilli Palmer (Lilli), Michael Redgrave (Army Captain)

Sabotage (1936)

Crew: *Director* Alfred Hitchcock, *Scenario* Charles Bennett, *Play* Campbell Dixon, *Novel The Secret Agent* Joseph Conrad, *Dialogue* Ian Hay & Jesse Lasky Jr. & Helen Simpson, *Additional Dialogue* E.V.H. Emmett, *Continuity* Alma Reville, *Producers* Michael Balcon & Ivor Montagu, *Original Music* Louis Levy, *Cinematographer* Bernard Knowles, *Film Editing* Charles Frend, B&W, 76 mins.

Cast: Sylvia Sidney (Winnie Verloc), Oskar Homolka (Mr Verloc), Desmond Tester (Mrs Verloc's Young Brother, Stevie), John Loder (Police Sergeant Ted Spencer), Clare Greet, Sara Allgood, Charles Hawtrey, Aubrey Mather

US Title: *The Woman Alone*

Young and Innocent (1937)

Crew: *Director* Alfred Hitchcock, *Scenario* Charles Bennett & Edwin Greenwood & Anthony Armstrong, *Dialogue* Gerald Savory, *Continuity* Alma Reville, *Novel A Shilling for Candles* Josephine Tey, *Producer* Edward Black, *Original Music* Al Goodhart & Al Hoffman & Samuel Lerner, *Cinematographer* Bernard Knowles, *Film Editing* Charles Frend, B&W, 80 mins.

Cast: Nova Pilbeam (Erica Burgoyne), Derrick de Marney (Robert Tisdall), Percy Marmont (Col. Burgoyne), Edward Rigby (Old Will), Mary Clare (Erica's Aunt), John Longden (Detective Inspector Kent), George Curzon (Guy), Basil Radford (Erica's Uncle)

US Title: *The Girl Was Young*

The Lady Vanishes (1938)

Crew: *Director* Alfred Hitchcock, *Screenplay* Sidney Gilliat & Frank Launder, *Novel The Wheel Spins* Ethel Lina White, *Producer* Edward Black, *Original Music* Louis Levy & Cecil Milner, *Cinematographer* Jack E. Cox, *Film Editing* R.E. Dearing, B&W, 97 mins.

Cast: Margaret Lockwood (Iris Henderson), Michael Redgrave (Gilbert Redman), Paul Lukas (Dr Hartz), Dame May Whitty (Miss Froy), Cecil Parker (Eric Todhunter), Linden Travers ('Mrs' Margaret Todhunter), Naunton Wayne (Caldicott), Basil Radford (Charters), Mary Clare (Baroness), Googie Withers (Blanche), Phillip Leaver (Signor Doppo), Catherine Lacey (The Nun)

Jamaica Inn (1939)

Crew: *Director* Alfred Hitchcock, *Adaptation* Alma Reville, *Dialogue* Sidney Gilliat, *Additional Dialogue* Joan Harrison & J.B. Priestley, *Novel* Daphne du Maurier, *Producers* Charles Laughton & Erich Pommer, *Original Music* Eric Fenby, *Cinematographers* Bernard Knowles & Harry Stradling Sr., *Film Editing* Robert Hamer, *Special Effects* Harry Watt, B&W, 100 mins.

Cast: Charles Laughton (Sir Humphrey Pengallan), Leslie Banks (Joss Merlyn), Emlyn Williams (Harr), Robert Newton (Jim Trehearne), Marie Ney (Patience), Wylie Watson (Salvation), Maureen O'Hara (Mary Yelland)

Rebecca (1940)

Crew: *Director* Alfred Hitchcock, *Adaptation* Philip MacDonald & Michael Hogan, *Screenplay* Robert E. Sherwood & Joan Harrison, *Novel* Daphne du Maurier, *Producer* David O. Selznick,

Original Music Franz Waxman, *Cinematographer* George Barnes, *Film Editing* W. Donn Hayes & Hal C. Kern, B&W, 130 mins.

Cast: Laurence Olivier (George Fortescu Maxmillian 'Maxim' de Winter), Joan Fontaine (The Second Mrs de Winter), George Sanders (Jack Favell), Judith Anderson (Mrs Danvers), Gladys Cooper (Beatrice Lacy), Nigel Bruce (Major Giles Lacy), C. Aubrey Smith (Colonel Julyan), Leo G. Carroll (Dr Baker)

Foreign Correspondent (1940)

Crew: *Director* Alfred Hitchcock, *Screenplay* Robert Benchley & Charles Bennett & Harold Clurman & Joan Harrison & Ben Hecht & James Hilton & John Howard Lawson & John Lee Mahin & Richard Maibaum & Budd Schulberg, *Producer* Walter Wanger, *Original Music* Alfred Newman, *Cinematographer* Rudolph Maté, *Film Editing* Dorothy Spencer, *Camera Operator* Burnett Guffey, *Special Production Effects* William Cameron Menzies, B&W, 120 mins.

Cast: Joel McCrea (Johnny Jones/Huntley Haverstock), Laraine Day (Carol Fisher), Herbert Marshall (Stephen Fisher), George Sanders (Scott ffolliott), Albert Bassermann (Van Meer), Robert Benchley (Stebbins), Edmund Gwenn (Rowley), Eduardo Ciannelli (Mr Krug), Harry Davenport (Mr Powers)

Mr & Mrs Smith (1941)

Crew: *Director* Alfred Hitchcock, *Screenplay* Norman Krasna, *Producer* Harry E. Edington, *Original Music* Edward Ward, *Cinematographer* Harry Stradling Sr., *Film Editing* William Hamilton, B&W, 95 mins.

Cast: Carole Lombard (Ann Krausheimer Smith), Robert Montgomery (David Smith), Gene Raymond (Jeff Custer), Jack Carson (Chuck Benson)

Bon Voyage (1944)

Crew: *Director* Alfred Hitchcock, *Screenplay* Angus MacPhail & J. O. C. Orton, *Subject* Arthur Calder-Marshall, *Technical Advisor & Dialogue* Claude Dauphin, *Cinematographer* Günther Krampf, B&W, 26 mins.
Cast: John Blythe, The Molière Players

Parker, *Producers* Frank Lloyd & Jack H. Skirball, *Original Music* Frank Skinner, *Cinematographer* Joseph A. Valentine, *Film Editing* Otto Ludwig, B&W, 109 mins.
Cast: Priscilla Lane (Patricia Martin), Robert Cummings (Barry Kane), Otto Kruger (Charles Tobin), Alan Baxter (Mr Freeman), Clem Bevans (Neilson), Norman Lloyd (Fry), Alma Kruger (Mrs Sutton), Vaughan Glaser (Mr Miller), Dorothy Peterson (Mrs Mason), Billy Curtis (Midget)

Shadow of a Doubt (1943)

Crew: *Director* Alfred Hitchcock, *Screenplay* Thornton Wilder & Sally Benson & Alma Reville, *Story* Gordon McDonell, *Producer* Jack H. Skirball, *Original Music* Dimitri Tiomkin, *Cinematographer* Joseph A. Valentine, *Film Editing* Milton Carruth, B&W, 108 mins.
Cast: Teresa Wright (Young Charlie Newton), Joseph Cotten (Charlie Oakley), Macdonald Carey (Jack Graham), Henry Travers (Joseph Newton), Patricia Collinge (Emma Newton), Hume Cronyn (Herbie Hawkins), Wallace Ford (Fred Saunders), Edna Mae Wonacott (Ann Newton), Charles Bates (Roger Newton)

Lifeboat (1944)

Crew: *Director* Alfred Hitchcock, *Screenplay* Jo Swerling & Ben Hecht, *Story* John Steinbeck, *Producer* Kenneth MacGowan, *Original Music* Hugo Friedhofer, *Cinematographer* Glen MacWilliams, *Film Editing* Dorothy Spencer, B&W, 96 mins.
Cast: Tallulah Bankhead (Constance Porter), William Bendix (Gus Smith), Walter Slezak (Willy, the German Submarine Commander), Mary Anderson (Alice MacKenzie), John Hodiak (John Kovac), Henry Hull (Charles D. 'Ritt' Rittenhouse), Heather Angel (Mrs Higgins), Hume Cronyn (Stanley Garrett), Canada Lee (George 'Joe' Spencer)

Suspicion (1941)

Crew: *Director & Producer* Alfred Hitchcock, *Screenplay* Samson Raphaelson & Joan Harrison & Alma Reville, *Novel Before the Fact* Francis Iles, *Original Music* Franz Waxman, *Cinematographer* Harry Stradling Sr., *Film Editing* William Hamilton, B&W, 100 mins.
Cast: Cary Grant (Johnnie Aysgarth), Joan Fontaine (Lina McLaidlaw Aysgarth), Cedric Hardwicke (General McLaidlaw), Nigel Bruce (Beaky), Dame May Whitty (Mrs McLaidlaw), Isabel Jeans (Mrs Newsham), Leo G. Carroll (Captain Melbeck)

Saboteur (1942)

Crew: *Director & Story* Alfred Hitchcock, *Screenplay* Peter Viertel & Joan Harrison & Dorothy

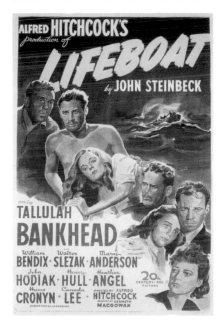

Aventure Malgache *(1944)*

Crew: *Director* Alfred Hitchcock, *Cinematographer* Günther Krampf, B&W, 31 mins.
Cast: The Molière Players

Spellbound *(1945)*

Crew: *Director* Alfred Hitchcock, *Screenplay* Ben Hecht, *Novel The House of Dr Edwardes* Francis Beeding, *Adaptation* Angus MacPhail, *Producer* David O. Selznick, *Original Music* Miklós Rózsa, *Cinematographer* George Barnes, *Film Editing* Hal C. Kern & William H. Ziegler, *Dream Sequence* Salvador Dalí, *Psychiatric Advisor* May E. Romm, B&W, 110 mins.
Cast: Ingrid Bergman (Dr Constance Peterson), Gregory Peck (Dr Edwardes/JB/John Ballantine),

Michael Chekhov (Dr Brulov), Leo G. Carroll (Dr Murchison), Rhonda Fleming (Mary Carmichael), John Emery (Dr Fleurot), Norman Lloyd (Garmes).

Notorious *(1946)*

Crew: *Director & Producer* Alfred Hitchcock, *Screenplay* Ben Hecht, *Original Music* Roy Webb, *Cinematographer* Ted Tetzlaff, *Film Editing* Theron Warth, *Second Unit Director of Photography* Gregg Toland, B&W, 100 mins.
Cast: Cary Grant (T.R. Devlin), Ingrid Bergman (Alicia Huberman), Claude Rains (Alexander Sebastian), Louis Calhern (Paul Prescott), Leopoldine Konstantin (Madame Sebastian)

The Paradine Case *(1947)*

Crew: *Director* Alfred Hitchcock, *Screenplay* James Bridie & Alma Reville & David O. Selznick & Ben Hecht, *Novel* Robert Hichens, *Producer* David O. Selznick, *Original Music* Franz Waxman,

Cinematographer Lee Garmes, *Film Editing* John Faure & Hal C. Kern, B&W, 132 mins.
Cast: Gregory Peck (Anthony Keane), Ann Todd (Gay Keane), Charles Laughton (Judge Lord Horfield), Charles Coburn (Sir Simon Flaquer), Ethel Barrymore (Lady Sophie Horfield), Louis Jourdan (André Latour), Alida Valli (Mrs Maddalena Anna Paradine), Leo G. Carroll (Council for the Prosecution)

Rope *(1948)*

Crew: *Director* Alfred Hitchcock, *Screenplay* Arthur Laurents & Ben Hecht, *Play* Patrick Hamilton, *Adaptation* Hume Cronyn, *Producers* Sidney Bernstein & Alfred Hitchcock, *Original Music* Leo F. Forbstein, *Additional Music* Francis Poulenc (from 'Perpetual Movement No. 1'), *Cinematographers* William V. Skall & Joseph A. Valentine, *Film Editing* William H. Ziegler, Colour, 80 mins.
Cast: James Stewart (Rupert Cadell), John Dall (Shaw Brandon), Farley Granger (Philip), Sir Cedric Hardwicke (Mr Kentley), Constance Collier (Mrs Atwater), Douglas Dick (Kenneth Lawrence), Edith Evanson (Mrs Wilson, the Governess), Dick Hogan (David Kentley), Joan Chandler (Janet Walker)

Under Capricorn *(1949)*

Crew: *Director* Alfred Hitchcock, *Screenplay* James Bridie, *Novel* Helen Simpson, *Producers* Sidney Bernstein & Alfred Hitchcock, *Original Music* Richard Addinsell, *Cinematographers* Paul Beeson & Jack Cardiff & Ian Craig & Jack Haste & David McNeilly, *Film Editing* A.S. Bates, Colour, 118 mins.
Cast: Ingrid Bergman (Henrietta Flusky), Joseph Cotten (Sam Flusky), Michael Wilding (Charles Adare), Margaret Leighton (Milly), Jack Watling

(Winter), Cecil Parker (Governor), Denis O'Dea (Corrigan)

Stage Fright *(1950)*

Crew: *Director & Producer* Alfred Hitchcock, *Screenplay* Whitfield Cook & Alma Reville, *Additional Dialogue* James Bridie, *Novel* Selwyn Jepson, *Original Music* Leighton Lucas, *Cinematographer* Wilkie Cooper, *Film Editing* Emard Jarins, B&W, 110 mins.
Cast: Marlene Dietrich (Charlotte Inwood), Jane Wyman (Eve Gill), Richard Todd (Jonathan/Jonny Cooper), Michael Wilding (Inspector Wilfred O. Smith), Alastair Sim (Commodore Gill), Sybil Thorndike (Mrs Gill), Kay Walsh (Nellie Goode), Miles Malleson (Bibulous Gent), Joyce Grenfell

(Shooting Gallery Attendant), André Morell (Inspector Byard), Patricia Hitchcock (Chubby Banister)

Strangers on a Train (1951)

Crew: *Director & Producer* Alfred Hitchcock, *Screenplay* Raymond Chandler & Whitfield Cook & Czenzi Ormonde & Ben Hecht, *Novel* Patricia Highsmith, *Original Music* Dimitri Tiomkin, *Cinematographer* Robert Burks, *Film Editing* William H. Ziegler, B&W, 101 mins.

Cast: Farley Granger (Guy Haines), Robert Walker (Bruno Anthony), Ruth Roman (Anne Morton), Leo G. Carroll (Senator Morton), Patricia Hitchcock (Barbara Morton), Marion Lorne (Mrs Anthony), Howard St John (Captain Turley), Jonathan Hale (Mr Anthony), Robert Gist (Hennessy), Laura Elliot (Miriam Haines)

I Confess (1953)

Crew: *Director & Producer* Alfred Hitchcock, *Screenplay* William Archibald & George Tabori, *Play Our Two Consciences* Paul Anthelme, *Associate Producer* Barbara Keon, *Original Music* Dimitri Tiomkin, *Cinematographer* Robert Burks, *Film Editing* Rudi Fehr, *Technical Advisor* Father Paul LaCouline, B&W, 95 mins.

Cast: Montgomery Clift (Father Michael Logan), Anne Baxter (Ruth Grandfort), Karl Malden (Inspector Larrue), Brian Aherne (Willy Robertson), O. E. Hasse (Otto Keller), Roger Dann (Pierre Grandfort), Charles André (Father Millais), Dolly Haas (Alma Keller), Ovila Légaré (Villette)

Dial M for Murder (1954)

Crew: *Director & Producer* Alfred Hitchcock, *Screenplay/Play* Frederick Knott, *Original Music* Dimitri Tiomkin, *Cinematographer* Robert Burks, *Film Editing* Rudi Fehr, Colour, 105 mins.

Cast: Ray Milland (Tony Wendice), Grace Kelly (Margot Wendice), Robert Cummings (Mark Halliday), John Williams (Inspector Hubbard), Anthony Dawson (Captain Swan/Lesgate)

Rear Window (1954)

Crew: *Director & Producer* Alfred Hitchcock, *Screenplay* John Michael Hayes, *Story* Cornell Woolrich, *Original Music* Franz Waxman, *Additional Music* Friedrich von Flotow (from '*Martha*'), *Cinematographer* Robert Burks, *Film Editing* George Tomasini, Colour, 112 mins.

Cast: James Stewart (L.B. 'Jeff' Jeffries), Grace Kelly (Lisa Carol Fremont), Wendell Corey (Thomas J. Doyle), Thelma Ritter (Stella), Raymond Burr (Lars Thorwald), Irene Winston (Mrs Thorwald)

To Catch a Thief (1955)

Crew: *Director & Producer* Alfred Hitchcock, *Screenplay* John Michael Hayes, *Novel* David Dodge, *Original Music* Lyn Murray, *Cinematographer* Robert Burks, *Film Editing* George Tomasini, Colour, 97 mins.

Cast: Cary Grant (John Robie), Grace Kelly (Frances Stevens), Jessie Royce Landis (Jessie Stevens), John Williams (H.H. Hughson), Charles Vanel (Bertani), Brigitte Auber (Danielle Foussard), Jean Martinelli (Foussard), Georgette Anys (Germaine)

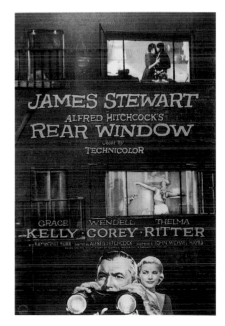

Cast: Cary Grant (Roger Thornhill), Eva Marie Saint (Eve Kendall), James Mason (Phillip Vandamm), Jessie Royce Landis (Clara Thornhill), Leo G. Carroll (The Professor), Philip Ober (Lester Townsend), Martin Landau (Leonard), Adam Williams (Valerian), Edward Platt (Victor Larrabee), Robert Ellenstein (Licht)

Psycho (1960)

Crew: *Director & Producer* Alfred Hitchcock, *Screenplay* Joseph Stefano, *Novel* Robert Bloch, *Original Music* Bernard Herrmann, *Cinematographer* John L. Russell, *Film Editing* George Tomasini, *Pictorial Consultant & Title Designer* Saul Bass, B&W, 109 mins.

Cast: Anthony Perkins (Norman Bates), Vera Miles (Lila Crane), John Gavin (Sam Loomis), Martin Balsam (Milton Arbogast), John McIntire (Sheriff Chambers), Lurene Tuttle (Mrs Chambers), Patricia Hitchcock (Caroline), Janet Leigh (Marion Crane), Virginia Gregg & Paul Jasmin & Jeanette Nolan (Voice of Mother)

The Birds (1963)

Crew: *Director & Producer* Alfred Hitchcock, *Screenplay* Evan Hunter, *Story* Daphne du Maurier, *Cinematographer* Robert Burks, *Film Editing* George Tomasini, *Electronic Sound Effects* Bernard Herrmann & Oskar Sala, Colour, 120 mins.

Cast: Tippi Hedren (Melanie Daniels), Rod Taylor (Mitch Brenner), Jessica Tandy (Lydia Brenner), Suzanne Pleshette (Annie Hayworth), Veronica Cartwright (Cathy Brenner), Ethel Griffies (Mrs Bundy), Charles McGraw (Sebastian Sholes), Ruth McDevitt (Mrs MacGruder), Lonny Chapman (Deke Carter)

The Trouble with Harry (1955)

Crew: *Director & Producer* Alfred Hitchcock, *Screenplay* John Michael Hayes, *Novel* Jack Trevor Story, *Associate Producer* Herbert Coleman, *Original Music* Bernard Herrmann, *Cinematographer* Robert Burks, *Film Editing* Alma Macrorie, Colour, 99 mins.

Cast: Edmund Gwenn (Captain Albert Wiles), John Forsythe (Sam Marlowe), Mildred Natwick (Miss Gravely), Mildred Dunnock (Mrs Wiggs), Jerry Mathers (Arnie Rogers), Royal Dano (Calvin Wiggs), Parker Fennelly (Millionaire), Barry Macollum (Tramp), Dwight Marfield (Dr Greenbow), Shirley MacLaine (Jennifer Rogers), Leslie Wolff (Art Critic), Philip Truex (Harry Worp)

The Man Who Knew Too Much (1956)

Crew: *Director & Producer* Alfred Hitchcock, *Screenplay* John Michael Hayes, *Story* Charles Bennett & D.B. Wyndham-Lewis, *Associate Producer* Herbert Coleman, *Original Music* Bernard Herrmann, *Songs* Ray Evans & Jay Livingston, *Cinematographer* Robert Burks, *Film Editing* George Tomasini, Colour, 120 mins.

Cast: James Stewart (Doctor Ben McKenna), Doris Day (Jo McKenna), Brenda De Banzie (Mrs Drayton), Bernard Miles (Mr Drayton), Ralph Truman (Buchanan), Daniel Gélin (Louis Bernard), Mogens Wieth (Ambassador), Alan Mowbray (Val Parnell), Hillary Brooke (Jan Peterson), Christopher Olsen (Hank McKenna), Reggie Nalder (The Assassin), Betty Bascomb (Edna), Bernard Herrmann (Himself, as conductor)

The Wrong Man (1956)

Crew: *Director & Producer* Alfred Hitchcock, *Screenplay* Maxwell Anderson & Angus MacPhail, *Book* The True Story of Christopher Emmanuel Balestrero Maxwell Anderson, *Associate Producer* Herbert Coleman, *Original Music* Bernard Herrmann, *Cinematographer* Robert Burks, *Film Editing* George Tomasini, *Technical Advisors* George Groves & Frank D. O'Connor, B&W, 105 mins.

Cast: Henry Fonda (Manny Balestrero), Vera Miles (Rose Balestrero), Anthony Quayle (Frank O'Connor), Harold Stone (Lt. Bowers)

Vertigo (1958)

Crew: *Director & Producer* Alfred Hitchcock, *Screenplay* Samuel A. Taylor & Alec Coppel, *Novel* The Living and the Dead Pierre Boileau & Thomas Narcejac, *Associate Producer* Herbert Coleman, *Original Music* Bernard Herrmann, *Cinematographer* Robert Burks, *Film Editing* George Tomasini, *Title Designer* Saul Bass, Colour, 128 mins.

Cast: James Stewart (John 'Scottie' Ferguson), Kim Novak (Madeleine Elster/Judy Barton), Barbara Bel Geddes (Marjorie 'Midge' Wood), Tom Helmore (Gavin Elster)

North by Northwest (1959)

Crew: *Director & Producer* Alfred Hitchcock, *Screenplay* Ernest Lehman, *Associate Producer* Herbert Coleman, *Original Music* Bernard Herrmann, *Cinematographer* Robert Burks, *Film Editing* George Tomasini, *Title Designer* Saul Bass, Colour, 136 mins.

Marnie (1964)

Crew: *Director & Producer* Alfred Hitchcock, *Screenplay* Jay Presson Allen, *Novel* Winston Graham, *Original Music* Bernard Herrmann, *Cinematographer* Robert Burks, *Film Editing* George Tomasini, Colour, 130 mins.

Cast: Tippi Hedren (Marnie Edgar), Sean Connery (Mark Rutland), Diane Baker (Lil Mainwaring), Martin Gabel (Sidney Strutt), Louise Latham (Bernice Edgar, Marnie's mother), Bob Sweeney (Cousin Bob), Mariette Hartley (Susan Clabon), Alan Napier (Mr Rutland), Bruce Dern (Sailor), Melody Thomas Scott (Young Marnie)

Torn Curtain (1966)

Crew: *Director & Producer* Alfred Hitchcock, *Screenplay* Brian Moore, *Original Music* John Addison, *Cinematographer* John F. Warren, *Film Editing* Bud Hoffman, Colour, 128 mins.

Cast: Paul Newman (Professor Michael Armstrong), Julie Andrews (Sarah Sherman), Lila Kedrova (Countess Luchinska), Hansjörg Felmy (Heinrich Gerhard), Tamara Toumanova (Ballerina), Wolfgang Kieling (Hermann Gromek), Ludwig Donath (Professor Gustav Lindt), Günter Strack (Professor Karl Manfred), David Opatoshu (Jakobi), Gisela Fischer (Dr Koska), Mort Mills (Farmer), Carolyn Conwell (Farmer's Wife)

Topaz (1969)

Crew: *Director & Producer* Alfred Hitchcock, *Screenplay* Samuel A. Taylor, *Novel* Leon Uris, *Associate Producer* Herbert Coleman, *Original Music* Maurice Jarre, *Cinematographer* Jack Hildyard, *Film Editing* William H. Ziegler, Colour, 126 mins.

Cast: Frederick Stafford (André Devereaux), Dany Robin (Nicole Devereaux), Karin Dor (Juanita de Cordoba), John Vernon (Rico Parra), Claude Jade (Michèle Picard), Michel Subor (François Picard), Michel Piccoli (Jacques Granville), Philippe Noiret (Henri Jarre), John Forsythe (Michael Nordstrom), Roscoe Lee Browne (Philippe Dubois), Per-Axel Arosenius (Boris Kusenov), Sonja Kolthoff (Mrs Kusenov), Tina Hedström (Tamara Kusenov)

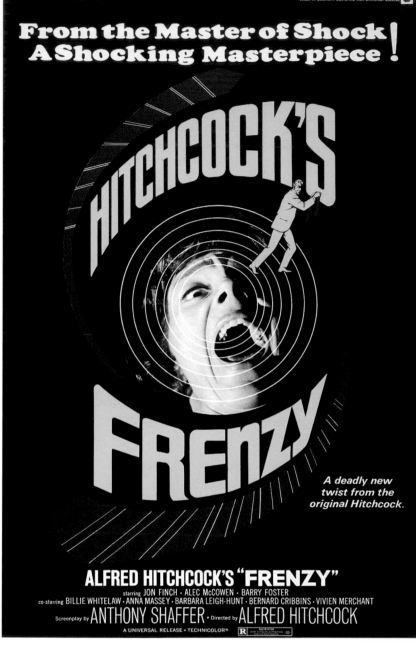

Frenzy *(1972)*

Crew: *Director & Producer* Alfred Hitchcock, *Screenplay* Anthony Shaffer, *Novel Goodbye Piccadilly, Farewell Leicester Square* Arthur La Bern, *Associate Producer* William Hill, *Original Music* Ron Goodwin, *Cinematographers* Leonard J. South & Gilbert Taylor, *Film Editing* John Jympson, Colour, 116 mins.

Cast: Jon Finch (Richard Blaney), Alec McCowen (Inspector Oxford), Barry Foster (Bob Rusk), Billie Whitelaw (Hettie Porter), Barbara Leigh-Hunt (Brenda Blaney), Vivien Merchant (Mrs Oxford), Anna Massey (Barbara 'Babs' Milligan), Bernard Cribbins (Felix Forsythe), Michael Bates (Sergeant Spearman), Jean Marsh (Monica Barling, Brenda's secretary)

Family Plot *(1976)*

Crew: *Director & Producer* Alfred Hitchcock, *Screenplay* Ernest Lehman, *Novel The Rainbird Pattern* Victor Canning, *Original Music* John Williams, *Cinematographer* Leonard J. South, *Film Editing* J. Terry Williams, Colour, 120 mins.

Cast: Karen Black (Fran), Bruce Dern (George Lumley), Barbara Harris (Blanche Tyler), William Devane (Arthur Adamson), Ed Lauter (Joseph Maloney), Cathleen Nesbitt (Julia Rainbird), Katherine Helmond (Mrs Maloney)

Bibliography

Bibliography
- Noble, Peter: *An Index to the Creative Work of Alfred Hitchcock*. Sight and Sound 1949
- Sloan, Jane E.: *Alfred Hitchcock: A Guide to References and Resources*. G.K. Hall 1993

Interviews with Alfred Hitchcock
- Bogdanovich, Peter: *Who the Devil Made it?* Alfred A. Knopf, 1997
- Cameron, Ian & Perkins, V.F.: 'Interview with Alfred Hitchcock'. Movie 6, January 1963
- Gottlieb, Sidney (ed.): *Hitchcock on Hitchcock: Selected Writings and Interviews*. Faber & Faber 1997
- Thomas, Bob (ed.): *Directors in Action*. Bobbs Merrill, 1973
- Truffaut, François & Scott, Helen G.: *Hitchcock*. Secker & Warburg 1967, revised Simon & Shuster 1984

Biographies, Memoirs, Analysis
- Allen, Richard & Ishii-Gonzalès, Sam. (eds.): *Alfred Hitchcock: Centenary Essays*. BFI 1999
- Auiler, Dan: *Hitchcock's Notebooks*. Spike 1999
- Auzel, Dominique: *Alfred Hitchcock*. Milan 1988
- Barr, Charles: *English Hitchcock*. Cameron & Hollis 1999
- Bouzereau, Laurent: *The Alfred Hitchcock Quote Book*. Citadel 1993
- Brill, Lesley: *The Hitchcock Romance: Love and Irony in Hitchcock's Films*. Princeton University 1988
- Brougher, Kerry & Tarantino, Michael (eds.): *Notorious: Alfred Hitchcock and Contemporary Art*. MOMA 1999
- Brown, Bryan: *The Alfred Hitchcock Movie Quiz Book*. Putnam 1986
- Chabrol, Claude & Rohmer, Eric: *Hitchcock*. Editions Universitaires 1957
- Cohen, Paula Marantz: *Alfred Hitchcock: The Legacy of Victorianism*. University of Kentucky 1995
- Condon, Paul & Sangster, Jim: *The Complete Hitchcock*. Virgin 1999
- Conrad, Peter: *The Hitchcock Murders*. Faber & Faber 2000
- DeRosa, Steven: *Writing with Hitchcock: The Collaboration of Alfred Hitchcock & John Michael Hayes*. Faber & Faber 2001
- Deutelbaum, Marshall & Poague, Leland (eds.): *A Hitchcock Reader*. Iowa State University 1986
- Douchet, Jean: *Hitchcock*. Cahiers du Cinéma 1999
- Duncan, Paul: *Alfred Hitchcock*. Pocket Essentials 1999
- Durgnat, Raymond: *The Strange Case of Alfred Hitchcock*. Faber & Faber 1974
- Freedman, Jonathan & Millington, Richard (eds.): *Hitchcock's America*. Oxford University 1999
- Freeman, David: *The Last Days of Alfred Hitchcock*. Overlook 1984
- Grams, Jr., Martin & Wikstrom, Patrik: *The Alfred Hitchcock Presents Companion*. OTR 2001
- Harris, Robert A. & Lasky, Michael S.: *The Complete Films of Alfred Hitchcock*. Citadel 1976
- Humphries, Patrick: *The Films of Alfred Hitchcock*. Brompton 1986
- Hunter, Evan: *Me and Hitch*. Faber & Faber 1997
- Jensen, Paul M.: *Hitchcock Becomes 'Hitchcock': The British Years*. Midnight 2000
- Kaganski, Serge: *Alfred Hitchcock*. Hazan 1997
- Kapsis, Robert E.: *Hitchcock: The Making of a Reputation*. University of Chicago 1992
- Kaska, Kathleen: *The Alfred Hitchcock Triviography & Quiz Book*. Renaissance 1999
- Krohn, Bill: *Hitchcock at Work*. Phaidon 2000
- LaValley, Albert J. (ed.): *Focus on Hitchcock*. Prentice-Hall 1972
- Leff, Leonard J.: *Hitchcock and Selznick*. Weidenfeld & Nicolson 1987
- McCarty, John & Kelleher, Brian: *Alfred Hitchcock Presents*. St. Martin's Press 1985
- Modelski, Tania: *The Women Who Knew Too Much: Hitchcock and Feminist Theory*. Methuen 1988
- Mogg, Ken: *The Alfred Hitchcock Story*. Titan Books 1999
- Narboni, Jean (ed.): *Alfred Hitchcock*. L'Etoile 1982
- Nevins, Jr., Francis M. & Greenberg, Martin H.: *Hitchcock in Prime Time*. Avon 1985
- Païni, Dominique & Cogeval, Guy: *Hitchcock and Art: Fatal Coincidences*. Centre Pompidou/Mazzotta 2001
- Perry, George: *The Films of Alfred Hitchcock*. Studio Vista 1965
- Price, Theodore: *Hitchcock and Homosexuality*. Scarecrow 1992
- Rothman, William: *Hitchcock: The Murderous Gaze*. Harvard University 1982
- Ryall, Tom: *Alfred Hitchcock and the British Cinema*. University of Illinois 1986
- Samuels, Robert: *Hitchcock's Bi-Textuality: Lacan, Feminism and Queer Theory*. State University of New York 1998
- Schickel, Richard: *The Men Who Made the Movies*. Atheneum 1975
- Sinyard, Neil: *The Films of Alfred Hitchcock*. Multimedia 1994
- Smith, Susan: *Hitchcock. Suspense, Humour and Tone*. BFI 2000
- Spoto, Donald: *The Art of Alfred Hitchcock: Fifty Years of His Motion Pictures*. Doubleday 1992
- Spoto, Donald: *The Dark Side of Genius: The Life of Alfred Hitchcock*. Ballantine 1983
- Sterritt, David: *The Films of Alfred Hitchcock*. Cambridge University 1993
- Taylor, John Russell: *Hitch: The Life and Times of Alfred Hitchcock*. Faber & Faber 1978
- Villien, Bruno: *Hitchcock*. Colona 1982
- Wolff, Mark H. & Nourmand, Tony: *Hitchcock Poster Art*. Aurum 1999
- Wood, Robin: *Hitchcock's Films Revisited*. Columbia University 1989
- Yacowar, Maurice: *Hitchcock's British Films*. Archon 1977

Books about Specific Films
- Auiler, Dan: *Vertigo: The Making of a Hitchcock Classic*. St. Martin's Press 1998
- Belton, John (ed.): *Alfred Hitchcock's Rear Window*. Cambridge University 1999
- Fawell, John: *Hitchcock's Rear Window*. Southern Illinois University 2002
- Leigh, Janet & Nickens, Christopher: *Psycho: Behind the Scenes of the Classic Thriller*. Harmony 1995.
- Paglia, Camille: *The Birds*. BFI 1998
- Rebello, Stephen: *Alfred Hitchcock and the Making of Psycho*. Marion Boyars 1998
- Ryall, Tom: *Blackmail*. BFI 1994
- Sharff, Stefan: *The Art of Looking in Hitchcock's Rear Window*. Limelight 1997

Screenplays
- Lehman, Ernest: *North by Northwest*. Faber & Faber 1999
- Anobile, Richard J. (ed.): *Alfred Hitchcock's Psycho*. Avon 1974

Documentaries
- AFI Life Achievement Awards: *Alfred Hitchcock*. Worldvision 1981
- Schickel, Richard: *The Men Who Made The Movies: Inside Hitchcock*. American Cinematheque 1973
- *Hitchcock, Selznick and the End of Hollywood*. American Masters 1998

Websites
- www.labyrinth.net.au/~muffin/ – The MacGuffin Webpage
- www.imdb.com

Notes

1. Thomson, David: *A Biographical Dictionary of Film*. André Deutsch, 1994
2. Overstreet, Richard: 'Interview with George Cukor.' Film Culture 34, Fall 1964.
3. Fontaine, Joan: *No Bed of Roses*, W.H. Allen, 1978.
4. Bogdanovich, Peter: *Who the Devil Made it?* Alfred A. Knopf, 1997
5. ibid.
6. Cameron, Ian & Perkins, V.F.: 'Interview with Alfred Hitchcock.' Movie 6, January 1963.
7. Taylor, John Russell: *Hitch: The Life and Times of Alfred Hitchcock*. Faber & Faber 1978
8. Thomas, Bob (ed.): *Directors in Action*. Bobbs Merrill, 1973
9. Kael, Pauline: *I Lost it at the Movies*. Little, Brown, 1963
10. Wolcott, James: 'Death and the Master.' Vanity Fair, April 1999
11. ibid.
12. see note 1
13. see note 8
14. Sarris, Andrew: *The American Cinema: Directors and Directions 1929–1968*. Dutton, 1969
15. see note 8
16. see note 14
17. Wood, Robin: *Hitchcock's Films Revisited*. Columbia University 1989
18. Spoto, Donald: *The Dark Side of Genius: The Life of Alfred Hitchcock*. Ballantine 1983
19. see note 8
20. see note 4
21. Greene, Graham: 'Review.' The Spectator, 11 December 1936
22. Greene, Graham: 'Review of Secret Agent.' The Spectator, 15 May 1936
23. ibid.
24. Truffaut, François & Scott, Helen G.: *Hitchcock*. Secker & Warburg 1967, revised Simon & Shuster 1984
25. Speech at Film Society of Lincoln Center, 29 April 1974
26. Gardiner, Dorothy & Walker, Kathrine Sorley (eds.): *Raymond Chandler Speaking*. Houghton Mifflin, 1977
27. Rodowick, David: 'Blackmail.' Cinema Texas Program Notes, 15 January 1979
28. Schickel, Richard: *The Men Who Made The Movies: Inside Hitchcock*. American Cinematheque 1973
29. Foster, Frederic: 'Hitch Didn't Want it Arty.' American Cinematographer, February 1957
30. Cameron, Ian (ed.): *Movie Reader*. Praeger, 1972

PAGE 192
Alma Hitchcock
Alma likes to keep her fridge well stocked.